Green

Gina **D. B. Clemen**

British and American Festivities

Editors: Victoria Bradshaw, Richard Elliott
Design and art direction: Nadia Maestri
Computer graphics: Simona Corniola
Illustrations: Simone Massoni
Picture research: Laura Lagomarsino

© 2004   Black Cat Publishing,
           an imprint of Cideb Editrice, Genoa, Canterbury

First edition: June 2004

Picture credits:
CONTRASTO: *Christopher Columbus* (1830-1871) by Jose Roldan © Archivio Iconografico, S.A: 7; *Haunted Halloween* © Chris Collins: 15; © Blue Lantern Studio: 18; © Azzara Steve: 19; *Postcard of Thanksgiving Dinner* (*c.* 1908) © Lake County Museum: 32; © Burnstein Collection: 34; © Kelly-Mooney Photography: 35; © Robbie Jack: 47; *Postcard of St Nicholas* © Rykoff Collection: 53; © Bettman: 54, 70, 90; © Owen Franken: 59 top left; © Marco Cristofori: 59 centre left; © Robert Essel NYC: 59 centre right; © Nevada Wier: 59 bottom left; © Mark Peterson: 62; © Neil Rabinowitz: 66; *King delivers his 'I have a dream' speech from the Lincoln Memorial, in Washington, DC* (1963) © Flip Schulke: 69, 76; © Morton Beebe: 77; © Douglas Peebles: 78; © Bequest of Mrs Benjamin Ogle Tayloe, Collection of The Corcoran Gallery of Art: *George Washington* (1796) by Gilbert Stuart 86, 88; © Joseph Sohm Visions of America: *The White House*, 87; © Philip Gould: *St Patrick's Day Participants throw Beads from Float* 95; © Szenes Jason: 96; © Sandy Felsenthal: 97; © Images.com: *Peaceful Dove* by Sue Truman 101; © Wally McNamee: 104; © David Cumming; Eye Ubiquitous: *May Day Celebration* 109, 124; © Gideon Mendel: 110, 111; © Francis G. Mayer: 118; © John Henley: 119. Bridgeman Art Library: Brooklyn Museum of Art, New York, USA: 8; Harrogate Museums and Art Gallery, North Yorkshire, UK: 27; Private Collection: 41, 116; Victoria & Albert Museum, London, UK: 46. Alamy: Alan Copson City Pictures: 43, 59 bottom right; lookGaleria: 60 top left; IMAGINA The Image Maker: 60 top right; Jon Arnold Images: 60 bottom left; picturescolourlibrary: 60 bottom right; Peter Bowater: 79; Robert Harding Picture Library: 123. Library of Congress, Prints and Photographs Division, Washington: 9, 10, 13, 33, 40. Getty Images / Laura Ronchi: 11, 44,45, 58 right, *Big Ben surrounded by fireworks at night* 61, 65, 84, 115. Mary Evans Picture Library: 16, *The Conspirators* (Guy Fawkes is No 6) 25, 26, 42, 74, *Popular Chinese street theatre commemorating the New Year* (19th century) 75, 106. ICP/TOPFOTO: 28. *The Choir* (late 19th century) by Paul Barthel © Christies Images 1987: 39. Granataimages: 49, 103. Foto Archivio APT Roma: 58 left. Congress – und Tourismus – Zentrale Nürberg: 59 top right. © S. J. Whitehorne / StillDigital: 63. FoodPix / Getty Images: 105. Yale University Art Gallery, Trumbull Collection: 117. www.britainonview.com: *Street Performer at Notting Hill Carnival* 122.
Extract from Dr King's speech (pp. 68, 71): reprinted by arrangement with the Estate of Martin Luther King Jr., c/o Writers House as agent for the proprietor New York, NY.
Copyright 1963 Martin Luther King Jr., copyright renewed 1991 Coretta Scott King.

We would be happy to receive your comments and suggestions, and give you any other information concerning our material.
editorial@blackcat-cideb.com
www.blackcat-cideb.com
www.cideb.it

CISQ CISQ CERT
TEXTBOOKS AND TEACHING MATERIALS
The quality of the publisher's design, production and sales processes has been certified to the standard of
UNI EN ISO 9001

ISBN 88-530-0193-3   Book
ISBN 88-530-0194-1   Book + CD

Printed in Italy

Contents

KET **Cambridge KET**-style exercises

T: GRADES 3/4 **Trinity**-style exercises (Grades 3/4)

The text is recorded in full.

These symbols indicate the beginning and end of the extracts linked to the listening activities.

Introduction

In this book you will learn about the most important festivities of the year in Britain and America, their origins and how people celebrate them. Here are some words and expressions you will find in various chapters of this book. How many of them do you know?

Things to see or do at festivities

• **a bonfire** :

• **to give cards** :

• **costumes** :

• **fireworks** :

• **flags** :

• **a float** :

• **to march** : soldiers walk in this way.

• **marching bands** : these groups of musicians march and play music in a parade (see below for 'parade').

• **a mask** :

• **a parade** : a celebration with a procession of people and floats in the streets.

• **to make a speech** : to talk formally about a subject in front of a group of people.

Historical background

- **bishop** : an important priest in the Christian Church (see below for 'priest').
- **Celts** (people) / **Celtic** (adjective) : these people originated in West and Central Europe in about 1200 BC. They came to the British Isles in the fifth century (see below for 'BC').
- **colonists** (people) / **colony** (place) : these people went to a different country and started living there. The new country became a colony of the original country they came from.
- **pagans** : these people believed in gods of nature. Pagan religions are older than the major religions of the world today.
- **priest** : this person performs religious ceremonies.
- **the Roman Empire** : this enormous empire included most of Europe, the Middle East and the north coast of Africa. It lasted from the first to the fifth centuries AD (see below for 'AD').
- **slaves** (people) / **slavery** (system) : these people were not free; a master owned them.

Times, days and measurements

- AD : abbreviation for *Anno Domini*. A way of counting the years after Christ was born.
- BC : abbreviation for *Before Christ*. A way of counting the years before Christ was born. Note: non-Christians sometimes use CE (Common Era) instead of AD, and BCE (before the Common Era) instead of BC. This system counts the years in the same way.
- **century** : 100 years.
- **mile** : 1 mile = 1.609 kilometres.
- **public holiday** : a national holiday.

Others

- **crops** / **harvest** : crops are plants that farmers grow for food. The harvest is the period of the year when the farmers collect the crops.

BEFORE YOU READ

1 **What do you know about Christopher Columbus? Choose the correct answer A, B or C.**

1. When was Columbus born?
   A ☐ 1351
   B ☐ 1451
   C ☐ 1551

2. What was his nationality?
   A ☐ Italian
   B ☐ Spanish
   C ☐ Portuguese

3. Which of these things did Columbus believe?
   A ☐ The world was square.
   B ☐ The world was flat.
   C ☐ The world was round.

4. Which continent did Columbus travel to?
   A ☐ America
   B ☐ Australia
   C ☐ Africa

2 **TRAVELLING BY SEA**

Do you know these words connected to travelling at sea? Match them to the correct definition.

a. to sail   i. To travel in order to find new places.
b. navigator   ii. To travel across an area of water.
c. ship   iii. This is a long journey at sea.
d. voyage   iv. This is the area where boats arrive and leave.
e. to explore   v. This is a large boat.
f. port   vi. This kind of explorer travelled by sea.

3 **GLOSSARY CHECK**

You can find definitions of the following words in the glossary on pages 4-5. Check any words that you do not understand.

- a float
- to march/marching bands
- a mile
- a parade
- costumes
- a colony

CHAPTER ONE

Columbus Day

On the second Monday of October Americans celebrate  Columbus Day; they remember Christopher Columbus's voyage to America in 1492.

Who was Christopher Columbus?

Christopher Columbus was born in 1451 in Genoa, a city on the north-west coast of Italy. At this time Genoa was a very important commercial port. The young Christopher often went to the port and watched the ships leave: they seemed to go under the horizon. [1] Many people at this time thought the world was flat, but others – Columbus included – believed that the world was round. Columbus wanted to test this idea. He first went to

---

1. **horizon** : where the sea and the sky meet.

sea when he was only fourteen years old.

Columbus went to live in Portugal. When he was only twenty-three he had the idea of going to India, China and Japan by sailing west. If the world was round, this was possible, he thought But he needed money, ships and men. He asked a lot of people for support, [1] including the kings of Portugal, England and France, but he got no help. Then he explained his idea to King Ferdinand and Queen Isabella of Spain. They were interested and, after some years, decided to help him.

Columbus before the Queen (1843) by Emanuel Gottlieb Leutze.

1. **support** [sə'pɔːt] : (here) financial help.

THE FIRST VOYAGE.

The first voyage (1893) by Prang Educational Company.

They gave him three ships: the *Santa Maria*, the *Niña* and the *Pinta*. It was difficult to find sailors for the voyage because it was long and dangerous. Finally, Columbus found about ninety men. He was ready to test his theory.

On 3 August 1492, Columbus and the sailors left Palos, on the coast of Spain. Queen Isabella and other important people went to see him leave.

Columbus navigated with a magnetic compass.[1] His ships travelled about 150 miles a day. The voyage was long and difficult, but the three ships arrived at the island of San Salvador in the Bahamas on 12 October 1492. Columbus claimed[2] these new lands for Spain.

Columbus's voyage changed the future of navigation, and the

1. **magnetic compass** :

2. **claimed** : said they were the property of Spain.

Columbus taking possession of the new country (1893)
by Prang Educational Company.

world. People in Europe called the new lands the 'New World'. When Columbus returned to Spain he told the King and Queen about the new lands and showed them gold, valuable objects and even some natives. They were very happy with Columbus's discovery.

After Columbus, people from other European countries also went to the New World. Spain, Portugal and England established colonies there. They found many new foods, plants and animals in the New World.

Celebrating Columbus Day

The first celebration of Columbus Day was on 12 October 1792, in New York City, three hundred years after Columbus's voyage.

Four hundred years after the discovery of the New World, the city of

Chicago celebrated Columbus's discovery with the Great Columbian Exposition. This exhibition, starting in May 1892 and finishing in October, attracted twenty-eight million visitors. Many streets, schools and universities all over the world are called 'Columbus'.

Today many Americans celebrate Columbus Day with colourful parades. There is also sometimes a kind of 'Miss Columbus', called a Columbus Day Queen. The parades are very long, with big floats dedicated to Columbus and marching bands. There are multicultural floats, too, and people of different nationalities participate in the parade.

Sometimes there are protests by groups of native Americans on Columbus Day. They remember that the arrival of Columbus meant the beginning of the domination of native Americans.

Columbus Day Parade in New York City.

UNDERSTANDING THE TEXT

1 **Are these sentences 'Right' (A) or 'Wrong' (B)? If there is not enough information to answer 'Right' (A) or 'Wrong' (B), choose 'Doesn't say' (C). There is an example at the beginning (0).**

0   People in the United States and Great Britain celebrate Columbus Day.
    A Right   (B) Wrong   C Doesn't say

1   Christopher Columbus came from Genoa.
    A Right   B Wrong   C Doesn't say

2   Columbus thought the world was flat.
    A Right   B Wrong   C Doesn't say

3   Columbus's father was a rich man.
    A Right   B Wrong   C Doesn't say

4   Columbus wanted to sail to the West.
    A Right   B Wrong   C Doesn't say

5   King Ferdinand and Queen Isabella gave Columbus a ship for the voyage.
    A Right   B Wrong   C Doesn't say

6   No one lived in the continent of America before Columbus arrived there.
    A Right   B Wrong   C Doesn't say

7   After Columbus, many other people explored the New World.
    A Right   B Wrong   C Doesn't say

8   The Italian population of San Francisco organized the first Columbus Day in 1792.
    A Right   B Wrong   C Doesn't say

9   Not all native Americans are happy about Columbus Day.
    A Right   B Wrong   C Doesn't say

2 **Which of these men were great explorers? Circle their names.**

| Marco Polo | King Arthur | Magellan | Robin Hood | Sir Francis Drake |
| Captain Cook | King Ferdinand | Vasco Da Gama | Amerigo Vespucci | |

Name a famous explorer from your country. ....
What countries or regions did he explore? ....

TOPIC – JOBS

Columbus became a great navigator. In a port like Genoa, many people worked on ships or at sea. What different jobs did people do in your town? What jobs do they do now? Think about a job you want to do. Bring a photo or picture of someone doing this job to the class and talk about it. Use the following questions to help you.

a. What job do you want to do?

b. Why do you like this job?

c. Is it interesting? Is it dangerous?

 Look at the picture and read the text below.

In 1893 the city of Chicago held the Great Columbian Exposition. The Exposition was on Lake Michigan.
It was a very important event for the city of Chicago. The city built many new, beautiful buildings. There were buildings to represent the different states of the United States of America and almost 50 foreign countries participated. Inside the buildings there was information about each state or country: its history, culture and art.

Now complete the sentences with the words from the box.

states	Lake Michigan	Chicago	information	buildings	countries

a. The Great Columbian Exposition was on .... in the city of
....

b. There were buildings to represent different .... and foreign
....

c. There was .... about each state or country inside the ....

BEFORE YOU READ

1 It is a Halloween tradition to make a 'jack-o-lantern'. Which vegetable do you think you use to make one?

A ☐ potato   B ☐ pumpkin   C ☐ turnip   D ☐ carrot

2 Do you know these popular Halloween foods? Match them to their names.

candied apples   liquorice   popcorn   pumpkin pie

A ....   B ....   C ....   D ....

3 Match these scary Halloween costumes to their names.

ghost   vampire   skeleton   witch

A ....   B ....   C ....   D ....

CHAPTER TWO

Halloween

October 31 is Halloween. It is a fun event in the United States, Great Britain and, now, in many other countries, too.

The Origins of Halloween

Halloween has Celtic origins. The Celtic calendar was in two parts: summer and winter. Summer was from May to the end of October, and winter was from November to the end of April. The ancient Celtic festivity Samhain [1] celebrated the end of the year: the start of winter. It began on the evening of October 31 and continued until the next day.

---

1. **samhain** : [saʊn].

Druidical ceremony at Stonehenge from
The costume of the original inhabitants of the British Isles (1815)
by Meyrick & Smith.

Druids were Celtic priests. On October 31 they performed religious rituals and talked about future events. The Celts believed that ghosts, witches and evil [1] spirits returned on the night of October 31. They believed that evil spirits entered the body of a person or animal. They wore frightening costumes and made big fires to send them away.

The colours of Halloween – orange and black – are of Celtic

1. **evil** : very bad.

origin, too. Orange was the colour of the harvest, and black was the colour of winter and long nights. The Druids believed that black cats had special powers and could feel if spirits were near. So black cats have become symbols of Halloween.

The Romans invaded Great Britain in AD 43. After this invasion Samhain became a harvest festival, and on October 31 the Romans honoured their goddess of fruit trees, Pomona.

During the centuries, the Roman Catholic Church put Christian festivities in the place of pre-Christian festivities. In the eighth century the Church decided to call 1 November All Saints' Day. Another name for this day was All Hallows'[1] Day. The evening of 31 October was All Hallows' Eve.[2] This became Halloween.

Celebrating Halloween Today

Halloween is celebrated in the USA, and has become popular in Europe, too. Many children and adults go to Halloween parties, wearing scary costumes and masks.

American children take their costumes and masks to school. Some typical Halloween costumes are witches, ghosts, skeletons, monsters, vampires and aliens. Many parents make the costumes, but some prefer to buy them. In the afternoon the children put on their costumes and have a Halloween party at school. Pumpkins, ghosts, witches and bats decorate the school hall and the classrooms.

There are, of course, party games. One is called 'bobbing for

1. **Hallows** : saints.
2. **Eve** : the day before a festivity.

Bobbing for Apples (early 20th century) by Clara M. Burd.

apples'. To play this game you put water and apples in a big bowl. The apples stay on top of the water. You must take an apple out of the water with your teeth, but you can't use your hands. It's not easy! Many people get very wet!

It is a popular tradition in the USA to buy a big pumpkin and make a jack-o'-lantern. People put their jack-o'-lanterns in front of the windows of their homes or in their gardens. This tradition originated in Great Britain and Ireland, when people wanted to frighten evil spirits. But they didn't use pumpkins then: they used big turnips. [1] In the United States there weren't any turnips, so

1. **turnips** : round vegetables (see page 14).

people used pumpkins.

Another popular Halloween tradition is 'trick or treating'. This began in the nineteenth century, and was an Irish tradition. Irish immigrants brought 'trick or treating' to the United States

Today children and teenagers go 'trick or treating' in the evening. They visit their neighbours' houses in their costumes. When the door opens they say 'Trick or treat?' People usually give them sweets or money. But when people don't give them a treat, the children play a trick. They sometimes write on windows with soap or even throw an egg at the front door of the house.

Halloween is not just for children. Many teenagers and adults wear costumes and go to parties on Halloween night.

A group of friends at a Halloween party.

UNDERSTANDING THE TEXT

 Choose the correct answer A, B or C. There is an example at the beginning (0).

0	When do we celebrate Halloween?	A ☐	On 1 November
		B ☑	On 31 October
		C ☐	On 30 October
1	What are the origins of Halloween?	A ☐	German
		B ☐	Irish
		C ☐	Celtic
2	When was Samhain?	A ☐	at the end of winter
		B ☐	at the beginning of the year
		C ☐	at the beginning of summer
3	Who were the Druids?	A ☐	Celtic witches
		B ☐	Roman priests
		C ☐	Celtic priests
4	What is 'bobbing for apples'?	A ☐	a Halloween game
		B ☐	a Halloween food
		C ☐	a Halloween costume
5	Who introduced the custom of 'trick or treating'?	A ☐	American children
		B ☐	Irish immigrants
		C ☐	the Romans

2 ***To scare*** **and** ***to frighten*** **have almost the same meaning. We use them to talk about something that makes us afraid. Look at their verb and adjective forms:**

VERBS : to scare, to frighten (*He frightened the old lady.*)

ADJECTIVES : scary, frightening (*I don't like that mask. It's scary!*)
to describe the way a person feels: *to be* + scared, frightened
(*She was scared.*)

Look at the sentences below. Do you need to use an adjective or a verb? Circle the correct word.

a. Evil spirits *scare/scary* me.

b. The haunted house is *frighten/frightening*.

c. Can we see your *scared/scary* costume?

d. The ugly mask *frightened/frightening* the small child.

e. This is a very *scare/scary* jack-o'-lantern!

f. Don't be *scare/scared*! It's only a costume.

Make a Jack-o'-lantern

1 Buy a big, round pumpkin.

2 Cut off the top of the pumpkin.

3 Use a spoon and clean the inside of the pumpkin.

4 Think of a funny or scary face. Then take a pen and draw the eyes, nose and mouth on the pumpkin.

5 With a knife, cut out the eyes, nose and mouth. Be careful!

6 Put a candle inside the pumpkin.

7 Put the jack-o'-lantern in front of a window, on your terrace or in your garden.

American PUMPKIN PIE

Invite your friends to a Halloween party. To make your party a big success, make an American pumpkin pie! It's delicious and easy to make! Here's a recipe for four people.

Ingredients

2 kg of pumpkin

1/2 litre of milk

4 eggs

1 cup of brown sugar

4 tablespoons of flour

1 teaspoon of baking powder [1]

100 g of butter

1/4 teaspoon of salt

1/4 teaspoon of cinnamon powder

Utensils to use

a big frying pan

a tablespoon

a teaspoon

a wooden spoon

a big bowl

a non-stick pie dish

1. **baking powder** : this helps the bread or cake mixture to get bigger in the oven.

1 Cut the pumpkin into small pieces and remove the peel. [1]

2 Put the pieces into a big frying pan and add the milk. Cook the mixture for 30 minutes. Don't forget to mix it.

3 Now break the eggs into a bowl. Add the flour, sugar, baking powder, butter, salt and cinnamon powder. Mix these ingredients.

4 Add the pumpkin and milk mixture to the ingredients in the bowl and mix.

5 Put the mixture into a non-stick pie dish and then put the dish into the oven (180 °C) for one hour.

6 Serve the pumpkin pie cold. Happy Halloween!

1. **peel** : (here) the skin of vegetables or fruit.

BEFORE YOU READ

1 **Match the words in the box to the correct picture.**

gunpowder   barrels   light the fuse

A ....   B ....   C ....

KET

2 **Listen to the beginning of Chapter Three. For questions 1-5, tick (✓) A, B or C.**

1   When is Guy Fawkes Night?   **A** ☐   on 5 November
                                 B ☐   on 15 November
                                 C ☐   on 25 November

2   Who passed laws   **A** ☐   King Henry VIII
    against Catholics?   **B** ☐   Guy Fawkes
                                 C ☐   King James I

3   Who wanted to destroy   **A** ☐   a group of Catholics
    Parliament?   **B** ☐   a group of priests
                                 C ☐   a group of the King's soldiers

4   What was the plot called?   **A** ☐   the Guy Fawkes Plot
                                 B ☐   the Bonfire Night Plot
                                 C ☐   the Gunpowder Plot

3 **GLOSSARY CHECK**

You can find definitions of the following words in the glossary on pages 4-5. Check any words that you do not understand.

- a bonfire   • costumes   • fireworks

CHAPTER THREE

Concilivm Septem Nobilivm Anglorvm Conivrantivm in Necem Jacobi I.
Magnæ Britanniæ Regis, Totivsq Anglici Convocati Parliementi.
1. Bates 2. Robert Winter 3. Christopher Wright 4. John Wright 5. Thomas Percy 6. Guide Fawkes 7. Robert Catesby 8. Thomas Winter

Guy Fawkes Night

Guy Fawkes Night is a British festivity. It takes place on 5 November.

Who was Guy Fawkes?

The Roman Catholic Church was the most important form of the Christian religion in England from the eighth century. The leader was the Pope, in Rome. But in 1534 the situation changed. King Henry VIII of England wanted to divorce his wife, Catherine of Aragon, because she could not have children, and marry another woman, Anne Boleyn. The Catholic Church did not permit this, so Henry VIII left the Roman Catholic Church and started the Church of England, with himself as its leader.

In 1605 the King – and leader of the Church of England – was

James I. He passed laws against Roman Catholics: they had to pay a lot of money if they did not go to Church of England religious services. A group of Catholics planned to blow up [1] Parliament in London on 5 November 1605, when the King was present. This plan was called the Gunpowder Plot. [2]

The leader of the plot was Robert Catesby. He and the others put thirty-six barrels of explosives under the Palace of Westminster. Guy Fawkes stayed there and waited to light the fuse.

But because of an anonymous letter the King's soldiers

Soldiers arrest Guy Fawkes under the Palace of Westminster.

1. **blow up** : explode.
2. **Plot** : a secret plan to do something bad.

Guy Fawkes before King James (1869-70) by Sir John Gilbert.

discovered the plot. They searched the Palace of Westminster and found Guy Fawkes with the explosives. They took him to the Tower of London. They wanted the names of the other men, but Fawkes did not speak. They then took Fawkes to King James I, but he still did not speak. Finally, they tortured him, and he told them everything. Soldiers went to arrest the other men, and killed some when they tried to escape. On 30 and 31 January 1606, they hanged [1] Guy Fawkes and another seven men from the plot.

1. **hanged** :

Celebrating Guy Fawkes Night

On the evening of 5 November there are fireworks and bonfires. Guy Fawkes Night is also called Bonfire Night.

Children often make a 'guy'. This is a model of Guy Fawkes. They use old clothes and fill them with newspaper, and they make a head and draw a face on it. They put the 'guy' on the bonfire and burn it.

Some people have bonfires in their gardens. But many people buy tickets and go to a public bonfire and firework display in their town or city. Children love the noise and the excitement.

On Bonfire Night in Lewes, Sussex, in south-east England, people wear historical costumes from the time of the Gunpowder Plot.

A bonfire on Guy Fawkes Night.

UNDERSTANDING THE TEXT

KET

 Read the text below and choose the best word (A, B or C) for each space. There is an example at the beginning (0).

In 1605 King James I passed (0) ....C.... laws against Roman Catholics living (1) .... England. Robert Catesby was (2) .... Catholic, and he and other Catholics (3) .... to destroy Parliament and kill the King.

They put thirty-six barrels of explosives (4) .... the Palace of Westminster. Guy Fawkes (5) .... the explosives. But the King's soldiers discovered the plot and found Guy Fawkes.

They took (6) .... to the Tower of London and later they hanged him (7) .... the other plotters.

Another name for Guy Fawkes Night is Bonfire Night. It is called this (8) .... in Great Britain people celebrate Guy Fawkes Night with big bonfires and fireworks.

0	**A** no	**B** any	Ⓒ new
1	**A** at	**B** in	**C** to
2	**A** a	**B** an	**C** the
3	**A** deciding	**B** decide	**C** decided
4	**A** over	**B** under	**C** at
5	**A** guarded	**B** guarding	**C** guards
6	**A** his	**B** he	**C** him
7	**A** and	**B** or	**C** but
8	**A** because	**B** for	**C** that

GRAMMAR CHECK

Use one of the question words in the box to complete each question. Then match the questions to the answers on the next page.

> Why   Who   How   What   When   Where

1. ☐   .... was the King of England in 1605?
2. ☐   .... did the plotters want to blow up Parliament?
3. ☐   .... many barrels of explosives were there?
4. ☐   .... did the soldiers arrest Guy Fawkes?
5. ☐   .... do the British do on Bonfire Night?
6. ☐   .... is Lewes?

29

a. There were thirty-six barrels of explosives.

b. In 1605 King James I was the King of England.

c. It is in Sussex, in the south-east of England.

d. They wanted to blow up Parliament on 5 November 1605.

e. Because they discovered the plot.

f. They go to firework displays and make bonfires in the garden.

 Read these rules about firework safety and then complete the sentences with a word from the box.

Firework safety

Fireworks are fun but they can be very dangerous! Do you know these rules about firework safety?

1. ALWAYS ask an adult to help you.
2. Keep fireworks in a closed box or tin.
3. NEVER put fireworks in your pocket or in your bag!
4. Use them ONE at a time.
5. Read the instructions carefully.
6. NEVER return to a firework after you light it – it could explode.
7. NEVER stand near the fireworks.
8. NEVER throw fireworks.
9. Keep all pets and animals INSIDE the house. The loud noise scares them.

pets   careful   firework   adult   pocket

a. Ask an ………… to help you.

b. Do not carry fireworks in your …………!

c. Do not leave your ………… outside the house.

d. Do not go near a ………… after you light it.

e. Remember: be ………… with fireworks because people can get hurt.

BEFORE YOU READ

 Look at the different types of food Americans eat at Thanksgiving. Match the words in the box to the correct picture.

pumpkin pie   corn   turkey   rice   cranberry sauce

A ……………………   B ……………………   C ……………………

D ……………………   E ……………………

 GLOSSARY CHECK

You can find definitions of the following words in the glossary on pages 4-5. Check any words that you do not understand.

- crops
- harvest
- a parade
- a float

Thanksgiving

Americans of all religions celebrate Thanksgiving on the fourth Thursday of November. Children do not go to school, and most businesses close for four days. People in Canada also celebrate Thanksgiving, but they celebrate it on the second Monday in October.

Thanksgiving is a special day for families, and people travel great distances to be with their families for this occasion.

Why is Thanksgiving an Important Day?

The tradition started with the 'Pilgrim Fathers'. They were the founders [1] of a colony in North America. These people were Puritans. [2] They were against the Church of England, and

---

1. **founders** : (from the verb to found = to establish) these are the first people to start to live in a new place.
2. **Puritans** : these people follow very traditional religious rules.

suffered religious persecution [1] in England. They wanted to start a new life in a new country.

Eventually, on 6 September 1620, 102 men, women and children left Plymouth in south-west England on a ship called the *Mayflower*. The voyage was difficult: two Pilgrims died, [2] but two were born. On 11 December 1620 they landed on the north-east coast of North America. They called this area Plymouth. It was almost winter and there wasn't much food. They immediately built small houses, but it was too late to grow crops. The winter was very long and cold and half of the Pilgrims died.

In the spring a native American called Squanto helped the Pilgrims. He taught them how to grow corn and how to hunt and

The landing of the Pilgrims on Plymouth Rock (c. 1846) by Sarony & Major.

1. **suffered religious persecution** : people treated them badly because of their religious beliefs.
2. **died** : (die, died, died) stopped living.

The first Thanksgiving by Jennie Augusta Brownscombe.

fish. Soon the Pilgrims and the Wampanoag [1] native Americans became friends. The Pilgrims grew crops and the summer harvest was excellent. By November 1621 everyone had food and a home. There was hope for the future.

William Bradford was the governor of the Pilgrim's colony. He decided to celebrate with a dinner for the Pilgrims and about ninety native Americans. He wanted to thank God. This was the first Thanksgiving dinner, and it continued for three days.

1. **Wampanoag** : [wɑːmpəˈnəʊəg].

A Traditional Thanksgiving

Today the traditional Thanksgiving meal is similar to the first. People eat roast turkey with cranberry sauce, potatoes, corn and pumpkin pie. Vegetarians don't eat meat, but they still celebrate Thanksgiving with other foods, such as soya products, rice, fruit, vegetables and big salads. Many charity organizations prepare a free meal for the poor people in their town or city.

New York City celebrates with Macy's Thanksgiving Day Parade. Macy's department store organised its first parade in 1924. This parade is very famous, and more than two million people go to see it every year.

A float in a Thanksgiving parade in New York City.

UNDERSTANDING THE TEXT

1 **Are the following sentences true (T) or false (F)? Correct the false ones.**

		T	F
a.	Canadians do not celebrate Thanksgiving.	☐	☐
b.	Americans celebrate Thanksgiving on the fourth Tuesday of November.	☐	☐
c.	The tradition of Thanksgiving started with the Pilgrims.	☐	☐
d.	There were only fifty people on the *Mayflower*.	☐	☐
e.	Their first winter in Plymouth was very difficult.	☐	☐
f.	The native Americans did not help the Pilgrims.	☐	☐
g.	The first Thanksgiving dinner continued for three days.	☐	☐
h.	The famous Macy's Thanksgiving Parade is in Los Angeles.	☐	☐

2 **Complete the crossword.**

1. Two .... people go to see Macy's Thanksgiving Parade.
2. The surname of the governor of the Pilgrims was ....
3. A long journey at sea.
4. These people established the new colony.
5. The name of the new colony.
6. Thanksgiving is on the fourth Thursday of ....
7. These native Americans helped the pilgrims.
8. Carrots, potatoes, corn etc.
9. Cruel treatment for religious or political beliefs.

What is the hidden word? ....

3 **You are Governor William Bradford. Complete this letter to your brother in England. Write only one word for each space.**

My dear Thomas,

It is difficult to believe we arrived (0) ..here. nearly one (1) .... ago. The voyage (2) .... the 'Mayflower' was terrible. We are lucky to be alive.

We have our own colony and you will not be surprised to know we call it Plymouth. Winter was very long (3) .... cold. But the natives here are friendly to us and they helped (4) ....

(5) .... the spring we started to grow crops. We even built small houses. We worked a lot and (6) .... harvest was good. Now we will celebrate (7) .... a big dinner (8) .... thank God for His help.

Your brother,

William

T: GRADE 4

4 **TOPIC – FOOD**

In this chapter you read about the special foods Americans eat at Thanksgiving. Work with a partner and talk about the special foods you eat during a festivity. Use these questions to help you.

a. What is the festivity?

b. What are the special foods?

c. Do you like these special foods?

d. Do you know how to prepare these foods? Who prepares them in your family?

BEFORE YOU READ

1 Here are some symbols of Christmas. Do you know them? Match the words from the box to the correct picture. Use your dictionary to help you.

Christmas stocking   elves   reindeer   present   holly
carol singing   mistletoe   sleigh   Christmas cracker

A ....

B ....

C ....

D ....

E ....

F ....

G ....

H ....

I ....

2 Do you celebrate Christmas? Do you have these symbols in your country? What other symbols do you have in your country?

CHAPTER FIVE

Christmas

Christians in many parts of the world celebrate Christmas on 25  December. This festivity celebrates the birth of Jesus Christ. Members of the Russian and Serb Orthodox Church celebrate on 7 January.

The History of Christmas

We do not know exactly when Christians first started to celebrate the birth of Christ. Many historians believe this was in the fourth century, when Christmas began to take the place of the pagan celebrations of the winter solstice, the shortest day of the year. The Bible does not say when Christ was born. Early Christians probably chose 25 December because it was near the dates of two pagan festivities.

The ancient Roman god of agriculture was Saturn, and in December the Romans celebrated Saturnalia. This festival lasted for many days and included the winter solstice. This day was usually on 21 or 22 December. During Saturnalia the Romans had parties and gave presents to their family, friends and children.

The pagan people of Scandinavia also had a winter festival. It was called Yule. It also included the winter solstice and lasted for many days. The men brought home a big log [1] and burnt it. They believed the log helped to bring back the sun. The family celebrated until the log stopped burning, and sometimes this took twelve days! Today, a popular cake at Christmas is in the form of a Yule log.

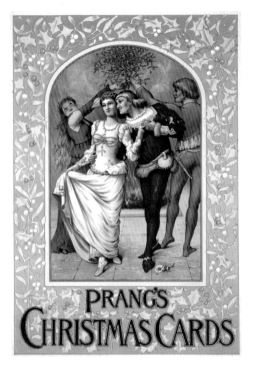

The traditions of Yule were fir trees, holly, mistletoe, cakes and presents. They are all still symbols of Christmas. Ancient Europeans believed that mistletoe had magic powers. Even today, if a boy and girl meet under the mistletoe they kiss. The tradition is that this brings good luck, and it is a sign of friendship and affection.

Today's traditional British

Prang's Christmas Cards. A couple kiss under the mistletoe (c. 1886).

2. log :

The Christmas Tree (1911) by Albert Chevallier Taylor.

Christmas comes from the Victorian period, when Victoria was queen (1837-1901). Christmas then started to become an important festivity. It was a time for the family to be together, and a time to enjoy special foods, music, carols and games. In Britain there were more things to buy in shops, and the tradition of giving presents grew. But at this time there were also big differences between the social classes: there were the very rich and the very poor. Rich children received dolls, dolls' houses, games and books. Poor children received an apple, an orange or a very small toy.

Charles Dickens described the Victorian Christmas in his *Christmas Stories*, especially in *A Christmas Carol* (1843). In this story Dickens shows the differences between the rich and the poor in Victorian society during Christmas celebrations.

Preparing for Christmas

When we think of Christmas we think of the Christmas tree. The tradition of the Christmas tree comes from Germany. Germans had a fir tree in their homes and they decorated it with biscuits and candles.

In Great Britain the Christmas tree became popular after 1840, when Queen Victoria married Prince Albert, a German. He brought the tradition of the Christmas tree to the Royal Family.

Prince Albert, Queen Victoria and the young Princess Royal and Prince of Wales admire the first Christmas tree at Windsor Castle (1842) by Alice Corkan

Then many people started to have Christmas trees in their homes.

Today almost every Christian family has a Christmas tree at home or in the garden. Some families put up the tree on Christmas Eve while many others put it up at the beginning of December. People decorate the tree with coloured lights and at the top of the tree they usually put an angel or a star. They also like to decorate their homes and gardens with other Christmas symbols such as holly, mistletoe and paper decorations. Towns and cities, too, usually decorate the trees in the parks with coloured lights.

Every year there is a very big Christmas tree in Trafalgar Square in London. It is a present from the people of Norway. This

The Norwegian Christmas tree in Trafalgar Square, London.

Christmas at the Rockerfeller Center in New York City.

tradition started in 1947, when the Norwegians wanted to thank the British for their help during World War II. This tree is about twenty-five metres tall and it is decorated with white lights.

America's most famous Christmas tree is at the Rockerfeller

Center on Fifth Avenue in New York City. This spectacular Christmas tree has about five miles of lights! Every Christmas millions of people go ice skating near the Rockerfeller tree.

Shopping for Christmas presents can be fun. During the Christmas season shops are open until late, and they are often open on Sundays, too. There are always a lot of people in the shops looking for the right presents for their family and friends. The shop windows have decorations, and many towns and cities put Christmas trees and other Christmas decorations in the shopping streets.

If you want to buy toys, in London there is a great toy shop called Hamleys. Children and adults love it: there are six floors full of toys and interesting games for all ages. Another wonderful toy shop is FAO Schwarz on Fifth Avenue in New York City. It is New York City's favourite toy shop.

Christmas decorations outside Harrods in London.

Christmas is a happy time, but it is also a time to help and remember others: no one wants to be alone at Christmas. During the Christmas season charity organizations ask for money for the poor people and the homeless in their town. They organize free meals and often give toys to the poor children.

In Great Britain and America people send Christmas cards to their friends and relatives; they usually buy boxes of Christmas cards, often from charity organizations. Many families show all the cards they receive: they put them on the walls in their houses. The British painter John Callcott Horsley designed the first Christmas card in 1843. The design was a family party with the words 'A Merry Christmas and a Happy New Year to you'.

Christmas carols and Christmas music are very popular. Many

The first Christmas card (1843) by John Callcott Horsley.

Christmas carols are very old. A lot come from Europe but some are American, too. People sing Christmas carols in church, in town centres and sometimes in front of their neighbours' houses. If people like the carols they give the carol singers money. The carol singers usually give this money to charity organizations.

In Great Britain pantomimes are very popular. This wonderful Christmas entertainment is a form of comic theatre, with songs. The stories are usually famous fairy tales such as *Cinderella*, *Sleeping Beauty* or *Aladdin*. A man usually acts the part of an old woman: this is a funny part. Pantomimes can be very noisy

A pantomime version of *Cinderella* at the Royal Opera House, Covent Garden, London, in 2003.

because the audience [1] participates in the performance a lot. The actors sometimes speak to the audience and the audience shouts an answer. The audience often sings with the actors, and when the 'bad' person of the story enters the audience says 'Boo!'. Pantomimes are lots of fun for all the family.

A Traditional Christmas Day

Some Christians go to church at midnight on Christmas Eve, while others go on Christmas morning. There are special Christmas services in all Christian churches. Some people don't go to church, but on Christmas Day families try to be together. People travel long distances to spend a family Christmas.

Children and adults usually open their presents on Christmas morning around the Christmas tree, or sometimes even in bed! This is a very happy moment, especially for the children.

In Great Britain there is a big Christmas lunch with special foods. People start cooking the Christmas meal very early, especially when there is a turkey. A big turkey takes a long time to cook.

Christmas crackers are an old tradition and are part of the Christmas lunch. Two people pull the cracker until it goes 'bang' and opens. Inside there is a small present, a paper hat and a joke. People sometimes wear the paper hat during the rest of Christmas lunch!

In the United States families spend Christmas Day together at

1. **audience** : these people watch the show.

home. They play games and watch Christmas films on television. In the evening they have a big Christmas dinner with lots of special foods.

On 26 December, St Stephen's Day in the Christian calendar, people in America go back to work, but in Britain, Canada, Australia and New Zealand they don't. In these countries 26 December is a public holiday; it is called Boxing Day. This name has two possible origins. Some say it has this name because in the past English masters gave their servants a box with small presents or money on 26 December. Others say it has this name because churches had boxes for the poor: people put money in these boxes, and the churches opened them on 26 December and gave the money to the poor.

UNDERSTANDING THE TEXT

1 **Are these sentences 'Right' (A) or 'Wrong' (B)? If there is not enough information to answer 'Right' (A) or 'Wrong' (B), choose 'Doesn't say' (C). There is an example at the beginning (0).**

0 No one knows exactly when Christians started celebrating Christmas.
(A) Right   **B** Wrong   **C** Doesn't say

1 In the fourth century Christmas began to replace pagan celebrations.
A Right   **B** Wrong   **C** Doesn't say

2 The Roman festival of Saturnalia began on December 25 and continued for seven days.
A Right   **B** Wrong   **C** Doesn't say

3 The pagan tribes of Scandinavia wore new clothes during Yule.
A Right   **B** Wrong   **C** Doesn't say

4 Holly, mistletoe, cakes and presents were the traditions of Yule.
A Right   **B** Wrong   **C** Doesn't say

5 Today's traditional Christmas comes from Victorian times.
A Right   **B** Wrong   **C** Doesn't say

6 In Victorian times no one gave Christmas presents.
A Right   **B** Wrong   **C** Doesn't say

7 The writer Charles Dickens wrote some stories about Christmas.
A Right   **B** Wrong   **C** Doesn't say

2 **Read the text below and choose the best word (A, B or C) for each space. There is an example at the beginning (0).**

The (**0**) ...B..... Christmas tree came (**1**) .... Germany and it became (**2**) .... during Queen Victoria's time. In Trafalgar Square in London there (**3**) .... a big Christmas tree. It comes from Norway. Most families today (**4**) .... a Christmas tree and decorate it with coloured lights.

People shop for Christmas presents (**5**) .... the Christmas season. Shops are open (**6**) .... late. There are Christmas decorations (**7**) .... In the weeks before Christmas people like sending Christmas cards to their friends and relatives.

Charity organizations (8) .... for money to help the poor people in their town. In Great Britain pantomimes are (9) .... of fun for all the family. The audience likes (10) .... in the noisy performance.

0	A present	B modern	C new
1	A from	B for	C at
2	A like	B favourite	C popular
3	A be	B is	C are
4	A have	B has	C having
5	A by	B at	C during
6	A until	B for	C since
7	A nowhere	B everywhere	C anywhere
8	A take	B make	C ask
9	A much	B lots	C lot
10	A participating	B participate	C participation

3 **Complete the spaces in this diary entry. Use the words in the box.**

> cooked   member   church   swim   water
> television   crackers   jacket   hats   presents

25 December

Today is Christmas Day! We went to (1) .... this morning. My uncle Edward didn't go to church because he went swimming! He is a (2) .... of the Serpentine Swimming Club in Hyde Park. Every Christmas morning the members of the club (3) .... for about 100 metres in the cold (4) .... of the Serpentine Lake. Mum thinks they're mad!

We opened our Christmas (5) .... before lunch. I got a game, two books and a blue (6) ....! I played with my new game all day.

Mum (7) .... a big turkey for Christmas lunch. There were lots of really nice things to eat. Grandma and Granddad came to lunch too. We pulled the Christmas (8) .... and we all wore our paper (9) .... during lunch.

After lunch Dad turned on the (10) .... and we watched a film. Grandma fell asleep.

Match a name (a-j) to the sentences (1-10).

a. Yule	f. Saturnalia
b. mistletoe	g. Charles Dickens
c. Prince Albert	h. Hamleys
d. John Calcott Horsley	i. pantomime
e. Trafalgar Square	j. Boxing Day

1. ☐ The Norwegians send a very big tree here.
2. ☐ The designer of the first Christmas card.
3. ☐ A famous British writer.
4. ☐ A British public holiday.
5. ☐ Ancient people believed it had magic powers.
6. ☐ A Scandinavian winter festival.
7. ☐ Queen Victoria's husband.
8. ☐ An ancient Roman festival.
9. ☐ Christmas entertainment at the theatre.
10. ☐ A famous toy store in London.

T: GRADE 3

5 TOPIC – HOME LIFE

On Christmas Day American families stay home and play games or watch television. Talk to another student about the things you do at home with your family.

a. What activities do you do at home with your family?
b. Does everyone in your family enjoy the same activities?
c. Which activities do you only do on special days or at weekends?

PROJECT ON THE WEB

Let's go carol singing!

Your teacher will give you the correct web-site address. Work in groups. Listen to some of the carols. You can even try and sing along. Which ones do you know? Do you sing them in your country? Which carols are your favourites?

Vive St. Nicolas

Father Christmas

Father Christmas, or Santa Claus, is based on St Nicholas. Nicholas was a Christian bishop of Myra (a town on the Mediterranean coast of modern Turkey) in the fourth century. He was famous because he was generous and kind. People started giving presents on his day in the Christian calendar, 6 December. Gradually this custom of giving presents moved to Christmas. But in some countries there was another traditional giver of presents: in England it was Father Christmas.

In the eighteenth century Dutch settlers took the tradition of Sinterklaas ('Saint Nicholas' in Dutch) to New York. The pronunciation of 'Sinterklaas' gradually became 'Santa Claus', and Santa Claus and Father Christmas became the same person.

The American cartoonist Thomas Nast created the modern image of Santa Claus in 1863. He is a happy old man with a white beard, wearing a red suit. He drives a sleigh pulled by reindeer, and comes down the chimney [1] with toys for children.

1. **chimney** :

Before American and British children go to bed on Christmas Eve, they leave mince pies, biscuits and something to drink for Father Christmas. They also leave a Christmas stocking, where Father Christmas puts their presents.

Merry Old Santa Claus (1881) by Thomas Nast.

Are these sentences true (T) or false (F)? Correct the false ones.

		T	F
1.	The modern Santa Claus comes from St Nicholas.	☐	☐
2.	St Nicolas's Day is on 25 December.	☐	☐
3.	Dutch settlers brought the tradition of Sinterklaas to Great Britain.	☐	☐
4.	Thomas Nast created the modern image of Father Christmas.	☐	☐
5.	On Christmas Eve American and British children leave an old shoe for Father Christmas.	☐	☐
6.	Father Christmas leaves presents in the chimney.	☐	☐

Christmas Foods

The traditional Christmas dinner consists of roast turkey and roast vegetables, followed by special desserts. Typical British desserts are Christmas pudding and mince pies, while in America fruit cake and pumpkin pie are popular. During the Christmas period other typical foods are roast ham, Yule logs and Christmas cake.

 Can you name these traditional Christmas foods?

Christmas cake   roast ham   roast turkey
Christmas pudding   mince pies   Yule log

A ....

B ....

C ....

D ....

E ....

F ....

How to Make a YULE LOG

Ingredients for the cake

2 eggs

100 g of white sugar

80 g of white flour

1 teaspoon of baking power

half teaspoon of salt

1 tablespoon of cocoa powder

1 teaspoon of vanilla extract

1 tablespoon of warm water

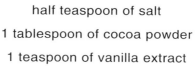

Ingredients for the chocolate butter cream icing

150 g of butter

150 g of sugar

cocoa powder

Mix the butter and sugar together well. As you mix, add some cocoa powder.

Utensils to use

fork

wooden spoon

cloth

baking tray

tablespoon

1 Break the eggs into a bowl and add the sugar.

2 Put the bowl over a saucepan of warm water and mix well. Add the water and the vanilla extract.

3 Mix the flour, baking powder, salt and cocoa powder with the egg and sugar mixture.

4 Put the mixture onto a baking tray. Then put it into the oven for 10-12 minutes at 200 °C.

5 Put the flat cake on a cloth and put some sugar around it.

6 Cover the flat cake with some of the chocolate butter cream icing.

7 Use the cloth and roll the flat cake carefully into a roll.

8 Put the chocolate butter cream icing on top of the log. Use a fork to make it look like a log.

9 Decorate it with holly or other cake decorations.

Christmas around the World

Christmas is different in different parts of the world. In the southern hemisphere it is summer in December, so Australians, for example have picnics on the beach and go swimming on Christmas Day.

In northern countries it is cold and there is the possibility of snow, a 'white Christmas'. In these countries there are a lot of traditional markets in December, where you can buy all kinds of Christmas decorations and presents.

Italy

Brazil

France

Germany

Spain

Japan

Mexico

Australia

Poland

Canada

Austria

Belgium

1 **Look at the twelve pictures and answer these questions.**

1. Which of these things can you find in the pictures? Use a dictionary to find the words you don't know.

> arch   barbecue   beach   clock   candles
> crackers   crib   dome   feathers   fountain   lights
> market   snow   star   surfboard   turkey

2. Choose one of the pictures and describe it to your partner. Do not tell them the name of the country. Your partner must guess the picture you are describing.

3. At Christmas, which of the countries in the pictures have hot weather and which have cold weather? What differences do you think there are in the way people celebrate Christmas in a hot country or in a cold country?

4. Choose one of the countries in the pictures. Find out more about how people celebrate Christmas in this country. Write about 100-150 words about Christmas in the country you choose.

CHAPTER SIX

New Year

New Year's Eve

The last day of the year, New Year's Eve, is on 31 December.
In America and Great Britain many people go to parties, restaurants or nightclubs. For some parties people wear costumes and masks. At midnight it is traditional to sing the old Scottish song 'Auld Lang Syne'. This song celebrates friendship.

In London lots of people go to Trafalgar Square and wait for the famous bell Big Ben to strike [1] midnight. Some people jump into the fountains!

---

1. **strike** : (here) make a loud noise typical of bells in clocks.

In New York City lots of people go to Times Square. At midnight the words 'Happy New Year' appear on an electronic sign. People cheer and there is a lot of noise.

In some American cities office workers throw their old calendars out of the windows on 31 December. They are throwing the old year away. By the evening there is lots of paper in the streets!

New Year's Eve celebration in Times Square.

Celebrating Hogmanay with a concert and fireworks below Edinburgh Castle.

In Scotland New Year's Eve is called Hogmanay. It is the most important celebration of the year for Scottish people. In Edinburgh and other cities people celebrate in the streets, and there are concerts and fireworks.

This is the time of year when people make 'New Year's Resolutions'. Resolutions are promises to change habits during the new year. Some typical resolutions are: 'I'm going to clean my

room regularly' or 'I'm going to do more sport'. Most people don't keep their resolutions, but some do!

New Year's Day

In many ancient civilizations the seasons controlled the calendar, and the New Year began on the first day of spring. But in 45 BC the Roman Emperor Julius Caesar created a new calendar. It was called the 'Julian' calendar, from 'Julius'. The first day of the new year became 1 January. The name 'January' comes from Janus, the Roman god of doors. Janus was therefore also the god of beginnings.

But the Julian calendar was not exact because it had 365 days. This was different from the solar year. [1] In 1582 Pope Gregory XIII corrected the Julian calendar and introduced the Gregorian calendar. He eliminated ten days from October that year: Friday 15 October 1582 was the next day after Thursday 4 October 1582! He also added an extra day to February every four years. This special year is called a leap year. It makes the calendar the same as the solar year.

Scotland started using the Gregorian calendar in 1600, but Great Britain and its colonies only started using it in 1752.

In Great Britain a lot of families have a special lunch and spend a quiet day at home. In the United States a lot of families have 'Open House' on New Year's Day. The first president of the United States, George Washington, introduced this tradition in the late 1700s. During 'Open House' the front door of your home is open all day. Friends and relatives come to visit. Many clubs and organizations have 'Open House' too.

---

1. **solar year** : the time the earth takes to go around the sun.

'Open House' in
the United States
on New Year's Day.

On New Year's Day it is cold in many parts of the United
States, but in California and many southern states it is warm and
sunny. In these places there are parades and American football
games. These football games, after the end of the normal football
season, are called bowl games. Each region has its parade and
bowl game.

The Pasadena 'Tournament of Roses' parade is a very colourful

Eagles on a float in the Pasadena 'Tournament of Roses' parade.

event. It started in 1890. There are about sixty spectacular floats in the parade every year. Colourful, beautiful flowers completely cover each float. There are figures of favourite characters from stories and famous people on the floats. The queen of this parade is called the Citrus Queen, because a lot of citrus fruits [1] grow in southern California.

Thousands of people go to watch the parade, and more than seventy million watch it on television. After the parade everyone goes to the football stadium to watch the Rose Bowl game.

1. **citrus fruits** : oranges, lemons, limes and grapefruits.

UNDERSTANDING THE TEXT

1 **Complete the sentences about New Year's Day. There is an extra ending that you do not need to use.**

1. ☐ In many ancient civilizations
2. ☐ Janus was the Roman god
3. ☐ The Gregorian calendar
4. ☐ Friends and relatives
5. ☐ In some American states
6. ☐ In Pasadena, California, there is

a. corrected the Julian calendar.
b. the 'Tournament of Roses' parade.
c. created the Julian calendar.
d. of doors.
e. the New Year began on the first day of spring.
f. come to visit during 'Open House'.
g. there are football games on New Year's Day.

2 **What New Year's Resolutions will you make this year? Make a list and discuss with the class.**

New Year's Resolutions 20_ _

1. ....
2. ....
3. ....
4. ....

T: GRADE 4

3 **Topic – Sports**

American football is a very popular sport in the United States. Do you have a favourite sport? Bring to the class a photo/picture of your favourite sport. Talk to your partner about this sport. Use the following questions to help you.

a. What is the name of the sport?
b. Describe the sport.
c. Is this sport popular in your country?
d. Do you do this sport, or are you a spectator?

BEFORE YOU READ

 What do you know about Dr Martin Luther King, Jr.? Discuss these questions with the class. Who was he? Where was he from? What did he believe? What did he do? When did he die?

Read this part of Dr King's famous speech.

> 'I have a dream that my four little children will one day live in a nation where they will not be judged by the colour of their skin but by the content of their character. I have a dream today.'

Now match these words to their meaning.

1. ☐ a dream	**a.** a country
2. ☐ a nation	**b.** a person's race or origins
3. ☐ to judge someone	**c.** a person's personality
4. ☐ the colour of someone's skin	**d.** a hope for the future
5. ☐ character	**e.** to form an opinion about someone

Complete the sentences with words from the box. Use your dictionary to check any words you don't understand.

> segregation   boycott   march   brutality

a. The black people of Montgomery, Alabama, decided to .... all buses. They didn't travel by bus for over a year.

b. Black children couldn't go to the same schools as white children because there was ....

c. Many policemen attacked the people. This was an example of police ....

d. In 1963, Dr King organized a big .... on Washington, DC.

CHAPTER SEVEN

Martin Luther King Day

On the third Monday in January America celebrates Martin
Luther King Day. This is quite a new public holiday in the United
States: it started in 1983.

Doctor Martin Luther King, Jr. [1] was an important person in the
American Civil Rights movement. He believed in non-violence.

Dr King was born on 15 January 1929 in Atlanta, Georgia and
became a Baptist minister. [2] At that time there was segregation in
the southern states of America. Black people could not use
certain types of public transport and go to the same schools and
churches as white people. Dr King didn't agree with this and he
protested in public. The police arrested him several times. On
one occasion John F. Kennedy asked the police to free Dr King.

1. **Jr.** : Junior. Some men use this title after their name if their father also
   has the same name.
2. **Baptist minister** : a religious leader in the Baptist Christian religion.

In many southern towns and cities, black people sat at the back of the bus and white people at the front. In 1955 in Montgomery, Alabama, one lady, Rosa Parks, refused to give her seat to a white person. The police came and arrested her. Dr King then organized a boycott of the Montgomery Bus System. No black person used a bus in Montgomery for 382 days. In the end the Supreme Court decided to stop segregation on public transport. After this victory Dr King was famous.

Martin Luther King, Jr. (front, centre) leads the march on Washington, DC, 28 August 1963.

After this there were many other victories. He campaigned against segregation and inequality in other cities in the South. In 1963 in Birmingham, Alabama he organized another peaceful protest. He invited children and young adults to march with him. The police commissioner, Eugene 'Bull' Connor, ordered his policeman to attack them with dogs and water cannons. Televisions and newspapers all over the world showed these pictures of police brutality.

In August 1963 Dr King helped to organize the Civil Rights march on Washington, DC. On that day he gave his most famous speech: everybody now knows the phrase 'I have a dream'.

These are some lines from that speech:

'I have a dream that my four little children will one day live in a nation where they will not be judged by the colour of their skin but by the content of their character. I have a dream today.'

In Washington, DC more than 200,000 people listened to this speech.

In 1964 America passed the Civil Rights Act. This changed the lives of African-Americans forever. In this year Dr King won the Nobel Peace Prize.

On 4 April 1968 a man called James Earl Ray assassinated Dr King in Memphis.

Every year Americans remember Dr King's work by celebrating this national holiday. All the schools close for the day. People try to remember what Dr King believed in. They try to help someone on this day. It is not a day for rest but a day to think about how we can help people around us. In 1969 Dr King's wife, Coretta Scott King opened the Martin Luther King, Jr. Center in Atlanta, Georgia. She wanted to help society change in a peaceful way.

UNDERSTANDING THE TEXT

1 **Are the following sentences true (T) or false (F)? Correct the false ones.**

	T	F
1. Americans celebrate Martin Luther King Day on the second Monday in January.	☐	☐
2. Martin Luther King Day started in 1983.	☐	☐
3. Martin Luther King was born in Memphis in Tennessee.	☐	☐
4. Martin Luther King was a Baptist minister.	☐	☐
5. There was segregation in all American states.	☐	☐
6. John F. Kennedy asked the police to arrest Dr King.	☐	☐
7. In 1961 Dr King organized the march on Washington, DC.	☐	☐
8. He believed in violence.	☐	☐
9. Martin Luther King won a Nobel prize.	☐	☐
10. Martin Luther King Day is a day of rest. Many people play sports.	☐	☐

2 **Dr King was born in *Atlanta*, Georgia; in 1963 Dr King helped to organize the March on *Washington, DC*; a man named James Earl Ray assassinated Dr King in *Memphis*.**
Do you know where these places are? Look at these descriptions and write the names in the correct boxes.

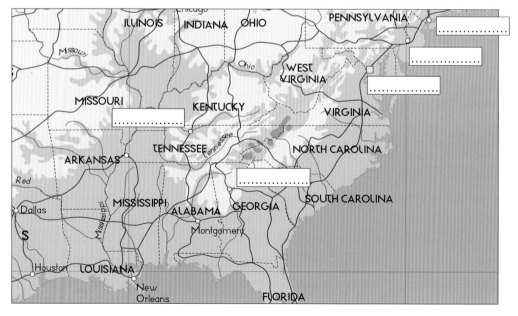

a. Memphis is in the south-central part of the United States. It is on the Mississippi River.

b. Washington, DC is on the East Coast of the United States, on the Potomac River, to the north of Virginia.

c. Atlanta is in the South East of the United States, above Florida.

d. New York City is on the north-east coast.

e. Philadelphia is in the East. It is between New York City and Washington, DC.

BEFORE YOU READ

1 **Look at this Chinese calendar. Write the names of the animals in the spaces.**

rat	tiger	snake	sheep	cockerel	pig
ox	dragon	horse	monkey	dog	rabbit

12. ....

11. ....

10. ....

9. ....

8. ....

7. ....

1. ....

2. ....

3. ....

4. ....

5. ....

6. ....

Look at the table below and answer these questions.

a. When were you born? Look for your birth year and find your Chinese Zodiac sign. What is it? …………

b. What is your best friend's sign? …………

 Read the characteristics of your sign. Are they true? Why or why not?

Rat **Years**: 1960 1972 1984 1996 **Character**: happy, charming, ambitious	**Horse** **Years**: 1966 1978 1990 2002 **Character**: popular, talkative, independent
Ox **Years**: 1961 1973 1985 1997 **Character**: works hard, patient, timid	**Sheep** **Years**: 1967 1979 1991 2003 **Character**: gentle, intelligent, loves beautiful things
Tiger **Years**: 1962 1974 1986 1998 **Character**: strong personality, courageous, temperamental	**Monkey** **Years**: 1968 1980 1992 2004 **Character**: intelligent, creative, solve problems easily
Rabbit **Years**: 1963 1975 1987 1999 **Character**: peaceful, sociable, secretive	**Cockerel** **Years**: 1969 1981 1993 2005 **Character**: faithful, punctual, eccentric
Dragon **Years**: 1964 1976 1988 2000 **Character**: energetic, honest, generous	**Dog** **Years**: 1970 1982 1994 2006 **Character**: loyal, honest, good leader
Snake **Years**: 1965 1977 1989 2001 **Character**: sensitive, responsible, careful with money	**Pig** **Years**: 1971 1983 1995 2007 **Character**: strong, kind, likes to learn

 GLOSSARY CHECK

You can find definitions of the following words in the glossary on pages 4-5. Check any words that are new or that you do not understand.

- BC
- costumes
- a float
- a mask
- fireworks
- a parade

CHAPTER EIGHT

Chinese New Year

Chinese New Year is a very important festivity for Chinese people  everywhere. It is also called the Spring Festival or the Lunar New Year.

The exact date of the Chinese New Year changes from year to year, but is always between 21 January and 19 February.

In ancient China people used the moon to calculate time, and in the Chinese lunar calendar every month begins with the new moon.

Every year of the Chinese Calendar has an animal's name. These animals are the rat, ox, tiger, rabbit, dragon, snake, horse, sheep, monkey, cockerel, dog and pig. The Chinese believe that a person born in a particular year has some of the characteristics of that animal.

Celebrating the Chinese New Year

Chinese families celebrate the new year for two weeks. They decorate their houses, towns and villages with coloured lanterns, flowers and many other decorations. They carefully clean the house and throw away old things. This means they are throwing away the bad luck [1] of the past year.

It is very important for the Chinese to be with their families on New Year's Eve. On this occasion the family eats a big, delicious meal together. Fish is always part of the dinner, along with rice, different meats, and vegetables. Each food has a special meaning, and the Chinese believe these foods bring good luck. On New Year's Day the Chinese wear new clothes to symbolize the New Year. Red is a popular colour because the Chinese believe that it is lucky. Parents and family members give children the traditional New Year's gift called 'Lai see' (lucky money): a red and gold envelope with some money inside.

1. **bad luck** : bad things that happen to you.

Lai see envelopes.

New Year's Day in San Francisco's Chinatown.

There are a lot of big Chinese communities outside China. In many big cities such as London, New York and San Francisco there are areas called 'Chinatown'. In these areas there are many Chinese shops and restaurants. Chinese New Year is a big celebration both for the Chinese and the local people of these areas, and there are a lot of colourful decorations in the streets of every Chinatown.

A Chinese dragon in a Chinese New Year parade.

A very important celebration is the parade on New Year's Day, when there are a lot of spectacular floats. The dragon is an important part of the parade because people believe it is noble and lucky. In the parade a dragon can sometimes be twenty-five metres long and can have about sixty men move under its body and tail! People often throw money at the dragon and the dragon tries to catch it in its big mouth. Sometimes there is more than one dragon in the parade. If so, there is a dancing competition between the dragons.

Lion dancing is an ancient Chinese tradition, and lion dancers are always part of the parade. Two men usually move under each lion. It has a big head and a long body. Musicians play the drums [1] and cymbals [2] during the lion dance. There are also noisy fireworks. The Chinese believe that the noise frightens evil spirits.

During the parade children represent the twelve animals of the Chinese calendar. Chinese children like wearing the costume of their favourite animal during the parade. There are also acrobats and musicians in beautiful costumes. Most of the costumes and masks in the parade come from China.

Chinese lion dancers.

1. **drums** :

2. **cymbals** :

UNDERSTANDING THE TEXT

KET

1 **Choose the correct answer A, B or C. There is an example at the beginning (0).**

0   Another name for Chinese New Year is
  A ☐ Winter Festival.
  B ✓ the Lunar New Year.
  C ☐ Lai see.

1   Chinese New Year is always
  A ☐ between 1 January and 19 February.
  B ☐ on 21 January every year.
  C ☐ between 21 January and 19 February.

2   In the Chinese Lunar calendar
  A ☐ every month starts with the new moon.
  B ☐ every month ends with the new moon.
  C ☐ every month starts the day before the new moon.

3   The Chinese celebrate New Year for
  A ☐ two days.
  B ☐ two weeks.
  C ☐ ten days.

4   On Chinese New Year's Day, Chinese children
  A ☐ play special games.
  B ☐ wear new clothes.
  C ☐ receive a lot of sweets.

5   'Lai see' is
  A ☐ a Chinese card.
  B ☐ a Chinese calendar.
  C ☐ an envelope with some lucky money.

6   The most important figure in the Chinese New Year parades is the
  A ☐ monkey.
  B ☐ dragon.
  C ☐ lion.

GRAMMAR CHECK

There are a lot of spectacular floats.

We use **a lot of** to mean a large number or quantity of something. We can also use **many** or **much** but these are more common in questions and negative sentences; they are not so common in affirmative sentences.

There were a lot of flags at the parade. There weren't many balloons.

Note: When we use **a lot of** for uncountable nouns (nouns we cannot count as separate objects: water, flour, money, etc.) the verb is in the singular form.

There is a lot of sugar in a pumpkin pie.

Look at the words in the box. Write C for countable or UC for uncountable next to each one.

present ☐   money ☐   vegetable ☐   rice ☐   snow ☐   lantern ☐

Now complete the sentences with the correct form of the verb *to be* and *a lot of*. You also need one word from the box above (make plurals if necessary).

Mum prepared rice with some fish for dinner. There were..... *also* .a.lot.of. *vegetables.*

a. Today is the start of Chinese New Year. There .... beautiful .... in the streets.

b. In some countries there .... in December and January.

c. There .... but we ate it all!

d. Look at all these envelopes! I hope there .... inside them.

e. There .... under the Christmas tree, ready for you to open.

BEFORE YOU READ

Listen to the beginning of Chapter Nine about Valentine's Day. Are these sentences true (T) or false (F)?

		T	F
a.	On Valentine's Day people celebrate by giving cards to people they love.	☐	☐
b.	The top of the Empire State Building has green lights on it on February 14.	☐	☐
c.	Lupercalia was a Celtic festival.	☐	☐
d.	Valentine secretly married young lovers.	☐	☐
e.	European immigrants took the Valentine tradition to America.	☐	☐
f.	People always sign Valentine cards with their names.	☐	☐

CHAPTER NINE

Valentine's Day

On 14 February lovers celebrate Valentine's Day. People in love give each other cards and presents: flowers – especially roses – chocolates or jewellery.[1] In the evening there are special parties, and couples sometimes go to restaurants for a romantic dinner. In New York City on the top of the Empire State Building there are red lights on Valentine's Day.

Where does Valentine's Day come from?

The ancient Roman festival of Lupercalia was on 15 February. On this day young men took the names of young women out of a vase. The couples formed in this way stayed together until the next Lupercalia. As usual, the Christian Church wanted to replace pagan festivals with Christian festivals. So, at the end of the fifth century Pope Gelasius created St Valentine's Day on 14 February.

1. **jewellery** :

Nobody knows exactly who Valentine was. There are three possibilities! Some people think he was a Christian priest when Claudius II was the Roman emperor. When he needed a lot of soldiers for his army Claudius did not permit marriages, [1] but Valentine performed marriages secretly. The authorities discovered this, and executed him in AD 270. There were another two Valentines in the third century: the Romans executed them because they were Christians. A legend says that one of them fell in love with the daughter of the prison keeper. Before his execution he wrote a letter to her: he signed [2] it 'from your Valentine'.

Valentine's Cards

European immigrants took the Valentine tradition to America. They made beautiful Valentine's cards. On the outside of the cards they painted butterflies, [3] flowers, cupids and hearts and on the inside they wrote original poems. In 1847 an American, Esther Howland, created the first commercial cards: people could then buy cards in shops.

Today few people make Valentine's cards: they buy them. Most cards are romantic, but some are humorous. In America many people also send cards to parents, relatives and friends as a sign of friendship. In Great Britain this is not common; Valentine's

---

1. **marriages** : ceremonies when a man and woman become husband and wife.

2. **signed** : wrote his name at the bottom of the letter.

3. **butterflies** :

cards are for lovers. However, the cards are usually anonymous – even between husband and wife! People don't sign their names: they sign the card with a question mark, or they do not sign the card at all.

In the United States young schoolchildren take to school the same number of Valentine's cards as the number of children in the class. There is no name on the envelope, but each child writes their name inside the cards. On Valentine's Day children make colourful red and pink decorations for their classroom, and the teacher gives the cards and some sweets to every child.

Young children 'posting' Valentine's cards at school.

UNDERSTANDING THE TEXT

1 **Complete the sentences with the correct word from the box.**

> presents   humorous   immigrants
> someone   cards   love   Roman   priest
> pagan   hearts   poems   friendship

a. On Valentine's Day people in love give each other .... and ....

b. Lupercalia was a .... festival.

c. The Christian church wanted to replace .... festivals with Christian ones.

d. Some people believe Valentine was a Christian .... at the time of the Roman empire.

e. European .... took the Valentine's tradition to America.

f. Before commercial cards people painted .... on cards and they wrote original ....

g. Some Valentine's cards are .... and others are romantic.

h. In America you can also give someone a Valentine's card as a sign of ....

i. Valentine's Day is an occasion to express .... or affection to .... special.

2 **GRAMMAR CHECK**

Use the prepositions in the box to complete the following sentences.

> to   for (x 2)   from   with   on (x 2)   in (x 2)

a. A young man took the name of a young lady .... a special vase.

b. Three Christian martyrs called Valentine lived .... the third century AD.

c. There are red lights .... the top of the Empire State Building.

d. People made beautiful cards with butterflies, flowers and hearts painted .... them.

e. In America people send cards .... parents, relatives and friends.

f. In the United States children take cards to school .... other children in their class.

g. People usually write an anonymous message .... the card.

h. Couples sometimes celebrate Valentine's Day .... a romantic dinner.

i. American children make Valentine decorations .... their classroom.

WORD PUZZLE

Do you remember these words? Complete the spaces with the correct letters.

1. an object to put flowers in
2. pretty metal or stones you wear
3. an ancient Roman festival
4. something funny or amusing
5. a beautiful insect

_ a _ _

j _ _ e _ _ _ r _

_ _ p _ _ _ _ _ i _

_ _ m _ _ o _ s

_ _ _ t _ r _ l _

BEFORE YOU READ

 KET

 Listen to the beginning of Chapter Ten about Presidents' Day and complete the table.

GEORGE WASHINGTON

1 George Washington was born on .... February .... in ....

2 At the age of twenty he became a .... with the .... army.

3 The War of Independence started in .... and ended in ....

4 George Washington was the .... of the American ....

5 In 1789, he became the .... of the United States.

6 He died in .... He was .... years old.

 GLOSSARY CHECK

You can find definitions of the following words in the glossary on pages 4-5. Check any words that are new or that you do not understand.

- colony/colonists
- to make a speech
- slavery/slaves

CHAPTER TEN

Presidents' Day

In the United States people celebrate Presidents' Day on the third Monday of February. This festivity celebrates the birthdays of two great presidents, George Washington and Abraham Lincoln.

George Washington

George Washington was born on 22 February 1732 in Virginia. At this time America was still a British colony.

At the age of twenty Washington became a soldier with the British army and fought against French colonists in America. In 1759 he married, and became the owner of a big plantation.[1] He also became interested in politics.

---

1. **plantation** : a big farm.

In 1765 the American colonists began to protest against Great Britain. They did not want to have British laws and pay taxes [1] to the British king, George III: they wanted America to become an independent nation. This was the beginning of the American Revolution.

1. **taxes** : you have to pay this money to the government.

George Washingto (1824) by Rembrandt Pea

The American War of Independence lasted from 1775 until 1783. For all this time Washington was the colonists' leader and commander of the American army.

Washington became the first president of the United States in 1789. He was dedicated and honest, and was president until 1797, when he chose not to accept a third Presidency. He retired from public life and two years later, in 1799, he died at the age of sixty-seven.

Abraham Lincoln

Another great president, Abraham Lincoln, was born on 12 February 1809 in Kentucky. As a child Lincoln only went to school for about a year, but he loved reading and studying: he wanted to learn.

When he was a young man Lincoln decided to enter politics in Illinois and also to study law. In 1836 he became a lawyer [1] in Springfield, Illinois. He also continued in politics, and in 1837 he became a member of Congress, [2] representing the state of Illinois.

Lincoln became the sixteenth president of the United States in 1861. At this time the question of slavery divided the North and the South of the United States: the South wanted slavery but the North did not. This was the most important cause of the American Civil War. This terrible war lasted from 1861 to 1865, and more than 600,000 soldiers died before the North won.

The Battle of Gettysburg was a very important victory for the North. It lasted three days in July 1863, and 40,000 soldiers died. On 18 November 1863 Lincoln went to Gettysburg to open the

---

1. **lawyer** : this person advises people about the law.
2. **Congress** : elected group of people, similar to Parliament in Britain. The American Congress makes laws.

Abraham Lincoln greeting African Americans by an unknown artist.

National Cemetery at the place of the battle. He gave a famous speech, called 'The Gettysburg Address', expressing the principles of democratic government. In his speech Lincoln used, for the first time, the famous expression 'government of the people, by the people, for the people.'

Soon after the end of the war, on 14 April 1865, Lincoln and his wife went to the theatre in Washington, DC. A man called John Wilkes Booth, a member of a Southern plot, shot and killed him. Lincoln was only 56 years old.

Presidents' Day is a national holiday. Many people put the American flag outside their homes, and some go to visit Washington's home in Virginia, or Lincoln's home in Illinois.

UNDERSTANDING THE TEXT

KET

1 **Read the text below and choose the best word (A, B or C) for each space. There is an example at the beginning (0).**

George Washington was born (**0**) ..B.. Virginia and lived on (**1**) ..... family's plantation. He became a soldier (**2**) ..... fought in the British army during a war against the French.

The American colonists chose Washington to be the (**3**) ..... of their army during the American Revolution. The colonists (**4**) ..... the war against Britain and America became an independent nation. George Washington became the first President of the United States of America.

Abraham Lincoln only went to school (**5**) ..... a year, but he wanted to learn so he continued to read many books. Later he decided to enter politics. He also became a famous lawyer. People liked and respected (**6**) ..... . He was President of the United States during the American Civil War. The North fought (**7**) ..... the South. President Lincoln passed a law against slavery. (**8**) ..... called it the Emancipation Proclamation. The North won the Civil War in 1865.

0	**A** on	**(B)** in	**C** at
1	**A** him	**B** he	**C** his
2	**A** and	**B** but	**C** yet
3	**A** director	**B** leader	**C** teacher
4	**A** won	**B** wins	**C** winning
5	**A** from	**B** to	**C** for
6	**A** his	**B** him	**C** he
7	**A** against	**B** to	**C** at
8	**A** She	**B** He	**C** It

PROJECT ON THE WEB

Let's find out about some presidents of the United States.

Your teacher will give you the correct web-site address.

Choose a president and click on his name.

Prepare a fact file on the president and present it to the class.

Complete the notes in the table about the life and times of Abraham Lincoln. When you finish, make full sentences using the Past Simple. If you chose a different president for your project on the Web, make a similar table with information about him.

Abraham Lincoln

Date	What happens
....	works as a lawyer
....	becomes congressman
1861	....
1861-65	....
....	man assassinates President Lincoln at the theatre

3 Rewrite these sentences in the correct order. There is an example at the beginning.

a. celebrate/Presidents' Day/February/Americans/in

   .Americans.celebrate.Presidents'.Day.in.February.....................

b. taxes/about/The colonists/protested

   ....

c. a/Washington/did/presidency/accept/third/not

   ....

d. fire/studied/the/by/Lincoln/in/evenings/the

   ....

e. the/was/Lincoln/during/Civil War/President

   ....

f. passed/slavery/He/law/a/against

   ....

g. homes/of/Many/Presidents/these/visit/Americans/the/two

   ....

4 Have fun with this crossword puzzle!

Across

3. The capital city of the United States of America is ………, DC.
4. A big battle of the American Civil War.
8. Lincoln only went to school for a year, but he wanted to ……… .
9. Young George Washington lived on a ……… .
11. Lincoln was born in the state of ……… .

Down

1. George Washington was the ……… of the colonists.
2. George Washington was born in the state of ……… .
5. Presidents' Day is celebrated in this month.
6. President Lincoln passed a law against ……… .
7. The name of the British king during the American Revolution.
10. Lincoln's job before he became President.

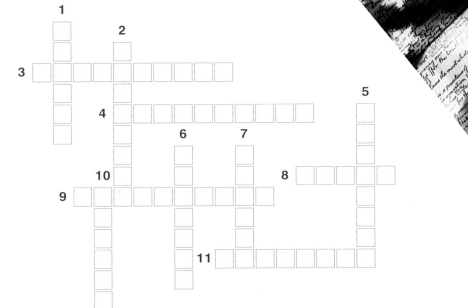

BEFORE YOU READ

1 Look at the pictures. Which ones are typically connected to Ireland and the Irish? Tick (✓) them.

A ☐ shamrock

B ☐ leprechaun

F ☐ rose

D ☐ Father Christmas

E ☐ wine

C ☐ whiskey

G ☐ the Tricolour flag

H ☐ the Union Jack

2 GLOSSARY CHECK

You can find definitions of the following words in the glossary on pages 4-5. Check any words that are new or that you do not understand.

- a slave
- a parade
- a priest
- to march/marching bands
- a flag
- a bishop
- Romans
- fireworks

CHAPTER ELEVEN

St Patrick's Day

St Patrick's Day on 17 March is the most important Irish festival.  Because of terrible conditions in Ireland during the 1800s many Irish went to America, so the Irish community in the United States is very big. They went to live all over the country and took their traditions with them. There are also many Irish in Britain, and all over the world.

Who was St Patrick?

St Patrick is the patron saint of Ireland. He was probably born in Wales, in about AD 389: his father was a Christian. When Patrick was sixteen years old some pirates [1] took him to Ireland, where he became a slave. After six years he escaped [2] to France. He became a priest there.

---

1. **pirates** : these people attack ships at sea and take things from them.
2. **escaped** : ran away (because he wanted to be free).

He returned to Ireland as a bishop in about 432. He converted a lot of Irish people to Christianity, and he introduced the Roman alphabet to Ireland. He wrote his autobiography in Latin about his life and work in Ireland. He died in about 461.

There are legends about St Patrick. One legend says he took all the snakes in Ireland to the top of a mountain and pushed them into the sea. Another legend says he used the shamrock to teach the Irish about Christianity: he used the three leaves of this plant to explain that for Christians God is three beings at the same time.

Celebrating St Patrick's Day

In Ireland St Patrick's Day is an important religious holiday. Businesses are closed and people go to church. In 1995 the Irish government started the St Patrick's Day Festival, a four-day festival in the capital city, Dublin. On St Patrick's Day there are a lot of tricolour flags in the streets. Irish people created this flag in 1848 with a special meaning. The green represents Irish Catholics (mostly from the south of Ireland) and the orange represents Irish Protestants (mostly from the north of Ireland). The white rectangle in the middle represents the hope for peace between

The Chicago River becomes green for St Patrick's Day.

Catholics and Protestants.

In the United States, the first celebration of St Patrick's Day was in Boston in 1737. Today on 17 March the Irish community in America organizes parades with marching bands and Irish music in many towns and cities. The parade in New York City is the biggest in the world: more than 150,000 people take part in the marching. And in the city of Chicago, the Chicago River is coloured green on St Patrick's Day!

The Irish believe that green is a lucky colour, and a lot of people wear green clothes on St Patrick's Day. The green shamrock is a symbol of Ireland, and another symbol is a leprechaun, a kind of Irish fairy. [1] This little old man usually wears green.

---

1. **fairy** : a fantasy character, not real. A fairy has magical powers.

UNDERSTANDING THE TEXT

1 **Are the following sentences true (T) or false (F)? Correct the false ones.**

	T	F
a. St Patrick's Day is on 17 March.	☐	☐
b. The Irish community in America is very small.	☐	☐
c. St Patrick is the patron saint of Ireland.	☐	☐
d. St Patrick became a priest in Ireland.	☐	☐
e. St Patrick brought Christianity to Ireland.	☐	☐
f. A legend says that St Patrick pushed the leprechauns in Ireland into the sea.	☐	☐
g. The orange part of the Tricolour represents the Irish Catholics.	☐	☐
h. Americans celebrated St Patrick's Day for the first time in 1737 in Boston.	☐	☐
i. Green is a lucky colour for the Irish.	☐	☐
j. On St Patrick's Day the river in Chicago becomes orange and green.	☐	☐

2 **Odd one out!**

Circle the word that doesn't belong.

a.	orange	green	colour	purple
b.	snake	bishop	fish	horse
c.	shamrock	leprechaun	rose	whiskey
d.	legend	tale	story	music
e.	France	Ireland	American	Britain

Now use the odd words to complete the sentences.

1. The band played traditional ....
2. My favourite .... is green.
3. Patrick became a ....
4. The .... is not a traditional symbol of Ireland.
5. The .... community in the United States is very big.

What nationality are people that come from the countries in the box? Look at the endings of the nationalities in the table below. Write each nationality in the correct column.

America	Australia	Canada	China	Denmark
England	France	Germany	Greece	Holland
Ireland	Italy	Japan	Norway	Poland
Portugal	Scotland	South Africa	Spain	Wales

-an	-ish	-ese	others
American	English	Chinese	Welsh
....	....	....	....
....	....	....	....
....	....		....
....	....		
....	....		
....			

Read about what these people do for some of the festivities you know about. From the information guess what nationality they are.

 a
 b
 c
 d
 e

a. New Year's Eve is one of the biggest celebrations of the year in Lisa's country. She likes to spend Hogmanay in her home town with her friends. ....

b. Sean celebrates his country's patron saint's day on March 17. Last year he spent a few days in the capital city because every year they organize special events. ....

c. James and Mark have a special dinner with their family in November. They love their grandma's pumpkin pie. ....

d. New Year is Chen's favourite time of year. It is a tradition in his country for relatives to give you little envelopes of money. His parents buy him new clothes. ....

e. Sarah and Lucy usually have a traditional dinner at home on Christmas Day. Their favourite part of Christmas is reading jokes from the Christmas crackers and watching old films.

....

BEFORE YOU READ

1 **What do you know about Easter?**

Match the words in the box to the correct picture.

> Easter Bunny   Easter egg   Easter bonnet

A ....   B ....   C ....

2
14 **Listen to the beginning of Chapter Twelve. Are the following sentences true (T) or false (F)?**

	T	F
1. Easter is a Christian celebration.	☐	☐
2. Easter is always on the last Sunday before the full moon in March.	☐	☐
3. The word Easter probably comes from the name of an old pagan goddess.	☐	☐
4. Pagans did not have eggs as symbols of new life.	☐	☐
5. Rabbits were symbols of fertility.	☐	☐

3 **GLOSSARY CHECK**

You can find definitions of the following words in the glossary on pages 4-5. Check any words that are new or that you do not understand.

- a parade
- pagans
- to march
- costumes

CHAPTER TWELVE

Easter

Easter is the most important festivity of the year for Christians. On Easter Day Christians celebrate the resurrection [1] of Jesus Christ. Easter Day is on the first Sunday after the full moon in March. This day is between 22 March and 25 April. The date is later in the calendar of the Eastern Orthodox Church.

Non-Christians like Easter time because some traditions remind people that nature is coming alive again after winter.

The Origins of Easter

The modern English word Easter may come from the name of an old northern European pagan goddess. The goddess with the most similar name was Ēastre, but there were other goddesses with names similar to Easter. They were all goddesses of spring

---

1. **resurrection** : coming back to life after being dead.

and fertility. [1] Pagans celebrated spring and the beginning of new life with festivals in March and April.

When Christianity became important, the Christian Easter gradually replaced pagan festivals. But we still use today some symbols from pagan spring festivals: flowers and eggs were symbols of new life, and rabbits were symbols of fertility.

Easter Today

For Christians the week before Easter is Holy Week. On Holy Thursday Christians remember the last meal Jesus had with his Disciples. [2] On Good Friday Christians believe that Jesus Christ died on the cross. [3] On Easter Day they believe that Jesus Christ came back to life, and went to heaven. [4] Many Christian families go to church on Easter Day in the morning.

There are also non-religious Easter traditions. One of these is wearing new clothes or new shoes. In America there are Easter Bonnet parades. Girls and women make their own original Easter bonnets and march in a parade. The famous Easter Bonnet Parade on Fifth Avenue in New York City is a tradition from the middle of the nineteenth century. Thousands of people go to watch it.

Easter Eggs and the Easter Bunny

In the days before Easter American and British schoolchildren sometimes paint Easter eggs with bright colours.

1. **fertility** : the ability to produce plants or children.
2. **Disciples** : the twelve men who followed Jesus Christ.
3. **cross** : ✝
4. **heaven** : in Christianity and some other religions, God lives in heaven. Good people go here when they die.

The Easter Bonnet parade in New York City.

Easter egg races in the White House gardens.

Immigrants from Germany brought the tradition of the Easter Bunny [1] to America. On Easter Day there are Easter egg hunts. [2] Parents hide eggs and ask their children to find them. The children go and look for the eggs. When they find them they put them in colourful Easter baskets. The child with the most eggs is the winner.

There are many games that you can play with eggs. For example, you can roll [3] eggs down a hill: the eggs must arrive at the bottom without breaking. On Easter Monday children from Washington, DC go the White House gardens and play all kinds of games with eggs. This tradition goes back to 1872, and the children of the President of the United States usually take part in the games.

1. **Bunny** : children's name for rabbit.
2. **hunts** : in a hunt you look for something.
3. **roll** : move by turning over and over.

Special Easter Foods

Families usually spend Easter Day together. The traditional Easter meal is roast lamb, new potatoes, peas and other vegetables.

There are chocolate eggs for children. Some eggs have a surprise in them, others have someone's name on them, and others... are just empty chocolate eggs!

Hot cross buns are typical on Good Friday in Britain. They are small, sweet cakes with a cross on top: the cross represents Jesus Christ's death on the cross.

Hot cross buns.

Events before Easter

Before Easter there is a period of time in the Christian calendar called Lent. It lasts for forty weekdays until Easter Day. During Lent some Christians do not eat some of their favourite foods. The day before Lent starts is called Shrove Tuesday. On this day the Christian tradition is to use all the fat foods in the kitchen before Lent begins.

Shrove Tuesday in Great Britain is also called Pancake Day because it is traditional to eat pancakes. [1] This is because pancakes use fat foods in the kitchen before Lent starts. In some places there are pancake races. People run and toss [2] pancakes in

1. **pancakes** : thin, soft, flat cakes made of flour, milk and eggs. They are usually served with lemon and sugar.
2. **toss** : throw in the air.

a frying pan. They must not drop the pancakes as they run.

Shrove Tuesday is called Mardi Gras in America. 'Mardi Gras' means 'Fat Tuesday' in French: the name refers to using fat foods before Lent. Mardi Gras is famous in America because of the carnival in New Orleans. Traditionally, carnival was a time of eating, drinking and fun before the serious period of Lent. In New Orleans there are celebrations and parades with amazing costumes for twelve days before Mardi Gras. Around three million people go to this carnival every year.

Pancake races on Shrove Tuesday (1949) by Walter Molino.

UNDERSTANDING THE TEXT

1 Choose the correct answer A, B or C. There is an example at the beginning (0).

0 German immigrants introduced
- **A** ☐ many Easter songs.
- **B** ☐ the Easter card.
- **C** ✓ the tradition of the Easter Bunny.

1 In New York City thousands of people participate in the
- **A** ☐ egg races.
- **B** ☐ big Easter egg hunt.
- **C** ☐ Easter Bonnet parade.

2 On Easter Monday in America there
- **A** ☐ is a traditional Easter egg hunt in every city and town.
- **B** ☐ are traditional egg games in the White House gardens.
- **C** ☐ is a concert in Central Park.

3 The British usually eat hot cross buns
- **A** ☐ on Holy Thursday.
- **B** ☐ on Good Friday.
- **C** ☐ on Easter Day.

4 During Lent, some people stop
- **A** ☐ eating some things they like.
- **B** ☐ playing games and going out.
- **C** ☐ doing things they don't like.

5 The carnival 'Mardi Gras' is in
- **A** ☐ New York.
- **B** ☐ Washington, DC.
- **C** ☐ New Orleans.

2 Let's go on an Easter egg hunt! Go through the maze and collect the eggs. Each coloured egg represents a letter of the alphabet and the eggs on the correct route will spell the answer to this question.

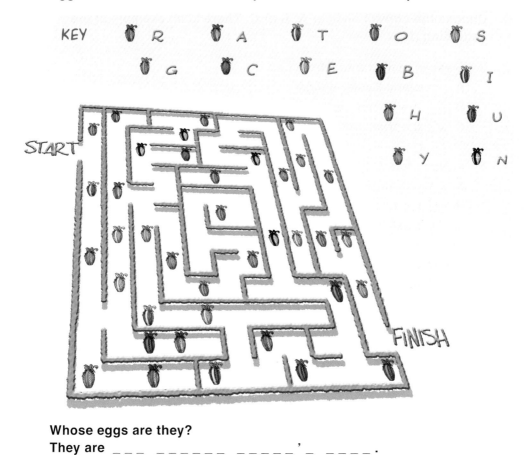

Whose eggs are they?

They are _ _ _   _ _ _ _ _ _   _ _ _ _ _ ' _   _ _ _ _ .

3 Test your memory! What happens on these days?

| Easter Sunday | Ash Wednesday | Shrove Tuesday | Good Friday |

BEFORE YOU READ

1 The words below are all in Chapter Thirteen about May Day. Can you guess what their connection is?

flowers   ribbons   dances   summer   public holiday

May Day

We celebrate the coming of summer on the first day of May. In
many countries 1 May is now a festival celebrating labour, [1] but
originally this day was a nature festival to celebrate new life and
welcome the warmer weather.

The Origins of May Day

Many ancient cultures had festivals at this time of the year.
The Celts celebrated the beginning of summer on the night
before 1 May. The name of this festival was Beltane. It was the
opposite of Samhain, the festival celebrating the beginning of
winter. On the night of Beltane the Celts made big bonfires.

At this time of the year the Romans had a festivity called

---

1. **labour** : work and physical effort.

Floralia in honour of Flora, the goddess of flowers and spring. When they invaded Britain they brought this festivity with them.

During the Middle Ages May Day was one of the most important days in the year. Everybody got up early and went 'maying': they went into the country to collect flowers and branches of trees to decorate their homes. Then there were games and singing and dancing. The most important dance was around the Maypole. People chose a girl from the village to be the 'Queen of the May'.

May Day Today

In Great Britain May Day is a public holiday. But it is not always on the first of May: it is on the first Monday in May. It is

Children dancing around the maypole.

Morris dancers at a May Day celebration.

much less important than in the Middle Ages, but there are still some traditions.

In traditional Maypole dances children dance around the Maypole. The Maypole, the ancient symbol of life, has many colourful ribbons [1] on it. The ribbons represent the rays [2] of the sun.

You can also see Morris dancing on May Day. This kind of dancing probably came from Spain in the fifteenth century, but it is a very British tradition now. Morris dancers dance with handkerchiefs [3] and bells. [4] They move their feet a lot to make the bells ring. This was to wake up the spirits in the earth after winter.

1. **ribbons** :   3. **handkerchiefs** :

2. **rays** :   4. **bells** :

UNDERSTANDING THE TEXT

 KET

1 **Are these sentences 'Right' (A) or 'Wrong' (B)? If there is not enough information to answer 'Right' (A) or 'Wrong' (B), choose 'Doesn't say' (C). There is an example at the beginning (0).**

0   The Romans were the first people to have a May Day Festival.
    (A) Right   B Wrong   C Doesn't say

1   In many countries May Day is a festival to celebrate work.
    A Right   B Wrong   C Doesn't say

2   The festivity continues for one week.
    A Right   B Wrong   C Doesn't say

3   Beltane was a Celtic festivity.
    A Right   B Wrong   C Doesn't say

4   In the Middle Ages to go 'maying' was to cut dry grass.
    A Right   B Wrong   C Doesn't say

5   An important event of May Day was a big dinner in the forest.
    A Right   B Wrong   C Doesn't say

6   The Queen of the May always wore white clothes.
    A Right   B Wrong   C Doesn't say

7   May Day is on 1 May in Great Britain.
    A Right   B Wrong   C Doesn't say

8   May Day is a public holiday in the United States.
    A Right   B Wrong   C Doesn't say

9   The Maypole has ribbons in different colours.
    A Right   B Wrong   C Doesn't say

10 Morris dancing probably comes from fifteenth-century Spain.
    A Right   B Wrong   C Doesn't say

 Answer these questions

    a. Is May Day a public holiday in your country? If it is, what do you do?
    b. Do you have special traditions for this day?

3 May Day celebrates the coming of summer. What things do you associate with the four seasons: spring, summer, autumn and winter? Work with a partner and think of at least five things for each season. Then tell the class. Do you all agree?

SPRING	SUMMER
....	....
....	....
....	....
....	....
....	....
AUTUMN	WINTER
....	....
....	....
....	....
....	....
....	....

KET

4 You will hear some information about the Beltane Fire Festival, which takes place on the night before May Day in Edinburgh. Listen to the information and complete the table.

BELTANE FIRE FESTIVAL

Date:	0 ...30 April...........
Time:	1 .... o'clock to .... o'clock
Place:	2 .... Hill
Events/attractions:	3 .... and ....
Cost of tickets:	4 £ ....
How to get there:	5 .... from Waverley Station
Safety points:	6 no glass .... / don't go near the ....

113

BEFORE YOU READ

1 **Listen to the beginning of Chapter Fourteen about Independence Day and for each question tick (✓) the correct answer A, B or C. There is an example at the beginning (0).**

0   Independence Day is on   A ☐   4 June.
                                 B ☐   14 July.
                                 C ✓   4 July.

1   In 1765 the thirteen American   A ☐   France.
    colonies belonged to   B ☐   Great Britain.
                                     C ☐   Spain.

2   The Boston Tea Party was   A ☐   an act of protest.
                                 B ☐   a social event.
                                 C ☐   an Independence Day party.

3   The American colonists   A ☐   wanted more English tea.
                                 B ☐   did not want to pay another tax.
                                 C ☐   did not want native Americans to
                                       have tea.

4   They read the Declaration   A ☐   in New York.
    of Independence   B ☐   in Boston.
                                 C ☐   in Philadelphia.

5   In 1783 America and Great   A ☐   in London.
    Britain signed a peace treaty   B ☐   in Paris.
                                     C ☐   in Boston.

6   Betsy Ross   A ☐   broke the Liberty Bell.
                                 B ☐   married George Washington.
                                 C ☐   made the first American flag.

2 **GLOSSARY CHECK**

You can find definitions of the following words in the glossary on pages 4-5. Check any words that you do not understand.

- colony/colonists
- a public holiday
- a flag
- a parade
- costumes
- fireworks
- to make a speech
- a century

CHAPTER FOURTEEN

Independence Day

The Fourth of July, or Independence Day, is 'America's birthday'. It is a public holiday, and Americans remember the ideals of liberty, equality, and opportunity for everybody.

The American Revolution

In the eighteenth century there were thirteen British colonies in America. But, starting in 1765, these colonies began to protest. They did not like paying high taxes to Great Britain, and they wanted America to become an independent nation with its own government. A number of different acts of protest against Great Britain started the American Revolution.

The Boston Tea Party is the most famous of these acts of protest. In 1773 the British Parliament put a new tax on tea. The American colonists were very angry: they did not want to pay

The Boston Tea Party (18th century) by an unknown artist.

another tax. So, on 16 December 1773, a group of colonists in Boston put on native American clothes, went onto three British ships, and threw 342 valuable boxes of tea into the sea.

The British Parliament reacted with severe laws, and the colonists protested even more. In April 1775 the American War of Independence began, with battles between British soldiers and American colonists at Lexington and Concord.

A group of fifty-six Americans – principally Thomas Jefferson, and including George Washington, Benjamin Franklin and others – wrote the Declaration of Independence. This document declared equality and liberty for all men, the separation of the thirteen American colonies from Great Britain, and the creation of the United States of America. On 4 July 1776 the leaders of the Revolution approved this document.

On 8 July 1776 they read the Declaration of Independence for the first time in public. This was in Philadelphia, Pennsylvania. After reading it they rang [1] a bell. It became a tradition to ring this bell every 4 July, until it broke in 1835. The bell, called the 'Liberty Bell', is still an important symbol of Independence Day: it is on display in the Independence National Historic Park in Philadelphia.

The war continued after the Declaration of Independence. The French took part on the side of the Americans in 1778, and in 1781 American and French soldiers won an important battle in Yorktown, Virginia. In 1783 America and Great Britain signed the final peace treaty in Paris, and the United States of America became an independent nation.

The Declaration of Independence, 4 July, 1776 (1776) by John Trumbull.

1. **rang** : (ring, rang, rung) made a sound typical of bells.

The American Flag

The American colonists wanted a flag for their new country. In 1776 Washington asked a friend, Betsy Ross, to make the first American flag. He showed Betsy a design of the new flag. There were thirteen red and white stripes, [1] and a circle of thirteen white stars on a blue background. The number thirteen was important because there were thirteen states in 1776. In June 1777 the new American flag was ready. Now there are fifty states and fifty white stars on the flag, but there are still only thirteen stripes. Americans call their flag 'The Stars and Stripes'.

Betsy Ross and the first 'Stars and Stripes' (1920) by John Ward Dunsmore.

1. **stripes :** ←

Independence Day Today

Today Americans celebrate 4 July in different ways. There is an American flag on public buildings and schools. Many people put a flag outside their windows or in their gardens. The flag is important to Americans; every morning, not just on Independence Day, schoolchildren salute the flag before they start the day's lessons.

Every city and town organizes celebrations, and there are red, white and blue decorations on the streets. Some traditional events are patriotic speeches, parades, baseball games, competitions, music, dancing, picnics, barbecues and fireworks. Picnics and barbecues are an American tradition, and at this time of the year people eat hamburgers, hot dogs, potato salad, chocolate cake and ice cream.

In the East there are historic parades with people in costumes from the eighteenth century. In the West there are spectacular rodeos, events where cowboys ride wild horses and catch young cows with ropes. There are also native American pow-wows – meetings of members of different tribes – and traditional dances.

American flags outside houses for Independence Day celebrations.

UNDERSTANDING THE TEXT

 KET

 Read the text and choose the best word (A, B or C) for each space. There is an example at the beginning (0).

The thirteen American colonies (0) A. to Great Britain at the beginning of the 1770s.
The American colonists paid (1) ..... taxes to Britain but they now wanted (2) ..... independence.
The British Parliament put a new tax on tea (3) ..... the colonists were very angry. Their act of protest was called the Boston Tea Party.
The colonists formed an army and fought (4) ..... the British. In 1783 America and Britain signed a peace treaty in Paris.
(5) ..... American patriots were Thomas Jefferson, Benjamin Franklin and John Adams. George Washington (6) ..... Betsy Ross to make the first American flag. (7) ..... the United States people celebrate Independence Day (8) ..... different ways.

0	(A) belonged	B were	C connected
1	A top	B high	C tall
2	A they're	B there	C their
3	A because	B and	C but
4	A against	B for	C with
5	A All	B Any	C Some
6	A said	B demanded	C asked
7	A In	B At	C On
8	A on	B in	C very

What did these people do? Read the questions and choose the correct name.

a. Betsy Ross
b. George Washington
c. Cowboys

d. The colonists
e. The British Parliament
f. Thomas Jefferson

Who:

1. ☐ threw tea into the sea at Boston?
2. ☐ wrote most of the Declaration of Independence?
3. ☐ made the first American flag?
4. ☐ put a new tax on tea?
5. ☐ celebrates Independence Day with rodeos?
6. ☐ was the first President of the United States?

GRAMMAR CHECK

Look at these sentences:

- *The colonists paid high taxes to Great Britain. There were acts of protests.*
- *The number thirteen was important. There were thirteen states in 1776.*

To join these sentences we use conjunctions. Common conjunctions are: **and**, **but**, **or**, **so** and **because**.

Now look at the joined sentences:

- *The colonists paid high taxes to Great Britain **and** there were acts of protest.*
- *The number thirteen was important **because** there were thirteen states in 1776.*

Rewrite these sentences choosing one of the conjunctions in brackets.

a. On 16 December a group of colonists went onto three British ships. They threw 342 boxes of tea into the sea. (*but/and/so*)

b. The American Revolution started. The American colonists wanted independence from Great Britain. (*but/so/because*)

c. The American Revolution started in 1775. It didn't finish until 1783. (*because/so/but*)

d. The Liberty Bell doesn't ring any more. In 1835 it broke. (*but/and/because*)

e. Every town organizes celebrations. There are decorations on the street. (*and/but/because*)

BEFORE YOU READ

 Listen to the beginning of Chapter Fifteen about the Notting Hill Carnival and complete the sentences.

a. Notting Hill Gate is an area in .... London.

b. The carnival is always on the Sunday and Monday of ....

c. Many of the original participants of this festival were from the islands of .... and ....

d. The first carnival in Notting Hill Gate was in ....

e. Before the carnival some participants make their beautiful .... and practise playing their steel ....

f. More than a .... people go to the see the carnival.

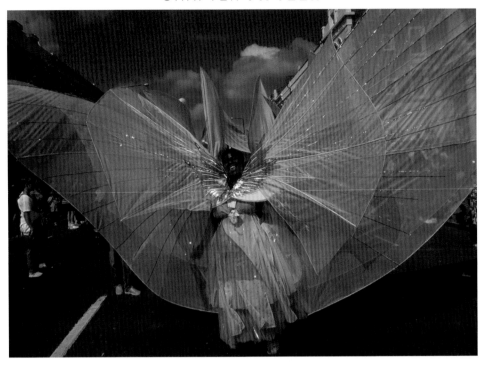

CHAPTER FIFTEEN

Notting Hill Carnival

The Notting Hill Carnival is the biggest street festival in Europe. It takes place in Notting Hill Gate, an area of west London, on the last Sunday and Monday of August. The last Monday of August is always a public holiday, so most people are free to come.

How did the Carnival start?

After World War II and during the 1950s people from the Caribbean, many of them from the islands of Trinidad and Tobago, came to Great Britain to work. They did not forget their traditions. Carnival was an important Caribbean tradition: the first Caribbean carnival took place in 1833 in Trinidad to celebrate the end of slavery.

In 1958 there was violence between white people and black

people in the Notting Hill area. The next year there was a decision to have a carnival to help black and white people in London to come together. It took place in different parts of west London, and in 1964 it took place in Notting Hill Gate.

There weren't many people in costume but they danced in the streets and played steel drums. [1] It was a great success. After 1964 it always took place in Notting Hill Gate.

The Carnival Today

Today the Notting Hill Carnival is an enormous multicultural festival. More than a million people go every year. Sunday is a family day, the best day for children to go.

Crowds of people watch the carnival in Notting Hill Gate.

1. **steel drums** : special metal drums. (These are typical musical instruments of the Caribbean.)

During the year the participants prepare for the carnival. They make their costumes, practise playing their steel drums, and prepare their floats.

On the days of the carnival, Notting Hill Gate is full of people, colour, excitement, music and noise. People with wonderful costumes dance in the streets. Steel bands play calypso, the traditional music of the Caribbean. They also play 'soca'. Soca is a newer form of music, a mixture of soul and calypso, but it is now associated with the carnival. There is also reggae, hip-hop and jazz.

There is a parade with colourful floats, and there is a prize for the best float. The parade travels about four and a half miles through the streets of West London.

And if you are hungry after all that dancing, you can find people selling meat and vegetable patties, [1] salted fish and other delicious Caribbean specialities.

1. **patties** : typical Caribbean food, similar to pies.

UNDERSTANDING THE TEXT

1 **Are the following sentences true (T) or false (F)? Correct the false ones.**

		T	F
a.	The Notting Hill Carnival is the biggest street festival in Europe.	☐	☐
b.	Notting Hill Gate is in East London.	☐	☐
c.	The first Caribbean carnival took place in Jamaica.	☐	☐
d.	The carnival is in a different area of London every year.	☐	☐
e.	The participants prepare for the carnival a long time before.	☐	☐
f.	People dance to different types of music at the carnival.	☐	☐
g.	The parade travels five miles through the streets of London.	☐	☐
h.	The best float receives a prize.	☐	☐
i.	Patties and salted fish are Caribbean specialities.	☐	☐

2 **Circle the words that are part of the Notting Hill Carnival.**

noise   school   boats   dragon   snow
steel drums   church   calypso   meat
April   costumes   parade   forest
police   salted fish   garden   dance
float   doctor   prize

Now use some of the circled words to complete the sentences.

a. The .... make a lot of ....

b. The .... travels four and half miles through the streets of London.

c. There is a .... for the best ....

d. You can eat .... patties and .... at the carnival.

e. People listen to the steel bands playing .... music.

f. Carnival groups wear beautiful .... and .... in the streets.

3 The adjectives in the box below can describe the nouns in exercise two (on page 125). Use these adjectives with the nouns and put them into the correct columns. You can use the adjectives more than once.

good   beautiful   delicious   long   short   loud
calypso   colourful   soca   wonderful

MUSIC	COSTUMES
....	....
....	....
....	....
....	....
....	....

PARADE	FOOD
....	....
....	....
....	....
....	....

KET

4 Complete this letter to your friend. Write one word for each space.

Dear Emma,

I went (0) ..to.............. the Notting Hill Carnival
yesterday. The carnival (1) .... wonderful and I had a
(2) .... of fun! There was music (3) ....
dancing in (4) .... streets. I saw a lot of beautiful
costumes and floats. Some people played steel drums.
There was also (5) .... long parade. The best float
(6) .... a prize.

I ate vegetable patties and salted fish. They (7) ....
delicious. Do (8) .... want to come with me next year?

Love,

Rob

EXIT **TEST**

1 **Match the description to the festivity.**

a. Columbus Day	f. Halloween	k. Guy Fawkes Night
b. Thanksgiving	g. Christmas	l. New Year
c. Chinese New Year	h. Valentine's Day	m. Presidents' Day
d. St Patrick's Day	i. Easter	n. May Day
e. Martin Luther King Day	j. Independence Day	o. Notting Hill Carnival

1. ☐ There is Morris dancing on this day.
2. ☐ The Pilgrim Fathers started this festivity.
3. ☐ The colour of this day is green.
4. ☐ A decorated fir tree is one of the symbols of this festivity.
5. ☐ On this day some people plotted to blow up Parliament.
6. ☐ This festivity celebrates an Italian navigator's voyage to the 'New World'.
7. ☐ The Scottish celebrate Hogmanay at this time of the year.
8. ☐ On this day Americans remember the dreams of an African-American.
9. ☐ Americans remember two famous presidents on this day.
10. ☐ The British eat hot cross buns during this festivity.
11. ☐ Jack-o'-lanterns and scary costumes are part of this fun festivity.
12. ☐ Some children receive special red envelopes at this time.
13. ☐ On this day Americans remember the American Revolution.
14. ☐ This is an enormous street festival in London.
15. ☐ On this day people can be romantic!

SCORE

2 **Are the following sentences true (T) or false (F)? Correct the false ones.**

	T	F
1. People make resolutions on New Year's Eve.	☐	☐
2. The Portuguese King and Queen gave Columbus three ships for his voyage.	☐	☐
3. Christmas is followed by Boxing Day in Great Britain.	☐	☐
4. Halloween has Roman origins.	☐	☐
5. Martin Luther King came from the North of the USA.	☐	☐
6. On Easter Monday children play games with eggs in the gardens of the White House.	☐	☐

		T	F

7. The 'Pasadena Tournament of Roses' is on the first day of the New Year in California. ☐ ☐

8. The Chinese think that red is an unlucky colour. ☐ ☐

9. A group of patriotic Americans wrote the Declaration of Independence on 4 July 1776. ☐ ☐

10. Guy Fawkes was the leader of the Gunpowder Plot. ☐ ☐

11. The origin of Valentine's Day is probably the Roman festivity of Lupercalia. ☐ ☐

12. St Patrick brought Christianity to Ireland. ☐ ☐

13. The Notting Hill Carnival takes place before Easter. ☐ ☐

14. The Pilgrim Fathers left Plymouth on a ship called the *Pinta*. ☐ ☐

15. The American Civil War was a war between the United States and Britain. ☐ ☐

SCORE

3 **What are these people famous for? Match the names with the events below.**

a. Betsy Ross
b. George Washington
c. St Valentine
d. King Ferdinand and Queen Isabella
e. Abraham Lincoln
f. Thomas Nast
g. St Patrick
h. Guy Fawkes
i. Prince Albert
j. William Bradford

1. ☐ He created the modern image of Santa Claus.
2. ☐ They helped Columbus with his plan to sail to the East.
3. ☐ He brought the tradition of the Christmas tree to Britain.
4. ☐ He was the governor of the Pilgrim Fathers' colony in America.
5. ☐ He was the first President of the United States.
6. ☐ He stayed with the explosives under Parliament in the Palace of Westminster.
7. ☐ He passed a law against slavery in America.
8. ☐ He secretly married couples when Claudius II was the Roman Emperor.
9. ☐ She made the first American flag.
10. ☐ He wrote about his life and work in Ireland – in Latin!

SCORE

TOTAL